1 Corinthians

1 Corinthians

A Pastoral Commentary

J. AYODEJI ADEWUYA
Foreword by Daniel K. Darko

WIPF & STOCK · Eugene, Oregon

1 CORINTHIANS
A Pastoral Commentary

Copyright © 2019 J. Ayodeji Adewuya. All rights reserved. Except for brief quotations in critical publications or reviews, no part of this book may be reproduced in any manner without prior written permission from the publisher. Write: Permissions, Wipf and Stock Publishers, 199 W. 8th Ave., Suite 3, Eugene, OR 97401.

Wipf & Stock
An Imprint of Wipf and Stock Publishers
199 W. 8th Ave., Suite 3
Eugene, OR 97401

www.wipfandstock.com

PAPERBACK ISBN: 978-1-5326-7400-6
HARDCOVER ISBN: 978-1-5326-7401-3
EBOOK ISBN: 978-1-5326-7402-0

Scripture quotations marked (NASB) are from the NEW AMERICAN STANDARD BIBLE®. Copyright © 1960, 1962, 1963, 1968, 1971, 1972, 1973, 1975, 1977, 1995 by The Lockman Foundation. Used by permission. All rights reserved.

Manufactured in the U.S.A.   MARCH 22, 2019

Contents

Foreword by Daniel K. Darko | vii

Preface | ix

	Introduction to 1 Corinthians	1
1 Corinthians 1:1–31	The Cross: God's Means of Salvation	9
1 Corinthians 2:1–16	Human Wisdom versus God's Wisdom	20
1 Corinthians 3:1–23	The Nature of Christian Leadership	28
1 Corinthians 4:1–13	The Nature of Christian Leadership Part 2	38
1 Corinthians 5:1–13	Discipline in the Church	45
I Corinthians 6:1–20	Christians in Pagan Courts	51
1 Corinthians 7:1–40	Marriage and Sexual Relations	60
1 Corinthians 8:1–13	Christian Liberty and the Common Good	68
1 Corinthians 9:1–27	Christian Privileges: Use and Abuse	75
1 Corinthians 10:1–33	Flee from Idolatry	84
1 Corinthians 11:1–34	Your Supper or the Lord's Supper?	94
1 Corinthians 12:1–31	One Body, Many Members	101
1 Corinthians 13:1–13	Love: The More Excellent Way	109
1 Corinthians 14:1–40	Spiritual Gifts and Edification	115
1 Corinthians 15:1–58	The Resurrection	124
1 Corinthians 16:1–24	Finance and Farewell	133

Further Reading | 139

Foreword

CHRISTIANITY IN THE TWENTY-FIRST century suffers from the amnesia of abundance to its own demise: abundance of books, scholars, moral problems, social stigmas, and leadership crises. Growing churches and Christian movements seem to have found no use for voluminous academic resources and erudite arguments by scholars on a wide range of Christian topics—often geared towards impressing peers in the guild. As if this is not enough, the blessings of technology have also led to information overload and engendered Biblical illiteracy simultaneously. PowerPoint presentations and creative endeavors of media departments in churches have inadvertently cultivated a sense of "no need for physical Bible" in the church or at home. Most Christians in the West have Bible apps, but know little about how the Bible may be applied to their lives. Professor Adewuya takes on his pastoral hat to make *1 Corinthians* come alive to the Christian who desires to study the letter in its context, be edified, and engage in learning experience for better Christian living. The interface of the author's academic acumen and pastoral passion draws the reader into a deep understanding and pragmatic learning experience on the multifaceted issues faced by the charismatic Christians in Roman Corinth. No footnotes. No Greek jargons. No big words. He seems to get what the average Christian needs. He writes as a pastor-scholar walking through the text with you and pointing to the way Paul addressed prevailing issues in the first century that resonate with ours today.

1 Corinthians: A Pastoral Commentary combines genres of commentary and devotion to foster a deeper understanding of God's word and Christian maturity. The book opens with biographical details of Paul and his ministry to set the tone and disposition with which Paul admonishes the urban Christians in Corinth. Identifying with the pastoral aims of Paul, Professor Adewuya articulates the sociohistorical background information

Foreword

concisely in non-scholarly parlance for the reader to grasp and relate to the commercial, religious, political, and even the backdrop of moral bankruptcy in the social location of Corinth. He aptly integrates up-to-date, scholarly findings in layman's terms—all with the aim to make the material accessible. Pastors and Bible study leaders would find salient, stimulating, and spiritually edifying discussions that meet the level of people at various social and education levels in the church. The commentary addresses division and its causes, partisan politics, sex and marital issues, orderly use of spiritual gifts and central doctrines such as the resurrection, clearly addressed with attention to how modern churches may engage and apply these admonitions.

Structurally, the book is invaluable in how it is organized, with a small number of pages allotted to each chapter. The subdivisions and comments are very engaging. The reflection or discussion questions at the end of the commentary on each of the sixteen chapters of 1 Corinthians makes it a useful resource for Bible studies or home groups whose members are too busy to read many pages but desire to grow in their knowledge of God's word. Adewuya's creative use of popular sayings, proverbs, and hymns appeal to relatable sensibilities and impress upon the heart the relevance of what Paul meant and what that would mean to the reader—that is how Paul's letter speaks to Christians today, personally and communally.

This is an excellent book bridging the gap between Biblical scholarship and church needs to grow in maturity and in numbers—providing useful insights, resources, and training in support of church ministries. The rare combination of brilliant scholarship and the unapologetic urge of an African pastor comes through the pages as a gift to the global church. I appreciate the depth and breadth, and the challenge it offers for spiritual maturity. It is spiritually edifying and refreshing to journey along with Professor Adewuya on tour, exploring what is going on in 1 Corinthians and how that may inform how we live as Christians. I commend him for this timely book and recommend the book for churches and home groups. It is an excellent resource.

Daniel K. Darko, PhD
Professor of New Testament
Gordon College, MA

Preface

My interest in Paul's letters to the Corinthians was kindled and grew during my graduate studies while serving as a missionary, pastor, and church-planter in the Philippines. A commentary of any sort was not in my dream at that time. That came about when I received an invitation to contribute a volume on 1 and 2 Corinthians to the International Study Guide Series by SPCK in London. That effort culminated in the publication of my book, *A Commentary on 1 & 2 Corinthians* in 2009. However, because of the constraint on the length of the book and other requirements by the publishers, especially format and style, I could not publish a commentary on 1 Corinthians as I would have wished¾a commentary that serves as a short historical and theological introduction for a non-academician, and that can be utilized as a devotional study guide both individually and corporately. This commentary is a realization of my desire.

Introduction to 1 Corinthians

ACTS 18:1–18 PROVIDES THE account of Paul's first visit to the Corinthians. His first canonical letter to the Corinthians offers a variety and wealth of material touching on Christian conduct, both for the individual and for the local church. Many of the problems in this book are rooted in the background and surrounding of the Corinthian believers. They needed to be established and grounded in God's word and, consequently, to live as befits their calling as God's people. The book is unique in its content, for beyond any other letter of Paul, one might say that it deals with an array and complexity of problems which might well find their parallel in today's world and churches.

THE WRITER

Paul's authorship of 1 Corinthians is hardly contested. In a manner typical of epistolary writing in antiquity, the writer identified himself at the beginning of the letter. At the time this letter was written, it was customary for the name of the writer to be placed at the beginning of the letter. The writer, Paul, was known among the early Christians as Saul the persecutor, whose name struck fear into the heart of believers. His conversion experience is narrated in Acts 9:1–6 and 15–16, and it is repeated in testimonies later (Acts 22:1–16). From the time Paul surrendered his life to Jesus Christ on the road to Damascus, his whole life was given to proclaiming the gospel, traveling as a missionary and establishing churches in many of the great cultural centers of the Greco-Roman world. Men and women who build, whether monuments or movements, are those who usually move under the force of great convictions. Paul was such a person. His life may be summed up in "Woe is me if I do not preach the gospel" (1 Cor 9:16).[1] It was such an inner urge and compulsion that brought him to the city of Corinth. Paul's ministry in Corinth was not underwritten, and such was his attitude toward money that he refused to take anything from them while he was in Corinth. Given the various problems at Corinth, ministers of lesser conviction would have quit. Not Paul. He was a man of passion who had a deep and abiding concern for the ones he had led to Christ. He wanted the best for them.

THE CITY OF CORINTH: ITS LOCATION AND HISTORY

A. Location

Corinth was a cosmopolitan city, a principal city of Greece and the capital of the province of Achaia. It was strategically located on the isthmus—that is, the narrow strip of land which connected northern and southern Greece and separated the Saronic and Corinthian gulf. It was the crossroad of East-West trade. It boasted of two major harbors; Cenchreae in the East and Lechaeum in the West. It controlled the north-south overland commercial traffic and the West-East sea route between Italy and Asia. Merchants preferred to unload their ships and transport their goods across the isthmus, while the empty ship went around the Pelopponese, the southern part of Greece, to avoid getting caught by one of the frequent dangerous storms and risking the loss of both their ships and cargoes. Corinth was a natural shipping and trading center.

B. History

The history of the city of Corinth has two parts. First, it was a city-state in the golden years of Athens. It flourished until the Romans destroyed it in 146 BC because of its refusal to submit to the demands of the Romans to dissolve the Achaean league, of which Corinth was a member. Second, in 44 BC, Julius Caesar rebuilt it as a Roman colony as part of Rome's plan to establish colonies to address overcrowding in cities and extend Roman civilization across the world. From 29 BC onward, it was the capital of the

---

1. Unless otherwise indicated, the NASB version of Scripture is used throughout this book.

senatorial province of Achaia and seat of the proconsul. The city retained this status until Paul's initial visit years later. Several things stand out about the city, as follows.

1. *Major Commercial Center.* Corinth was one of the busiest international ports of the ancient world.
2. *Political Center.* As the seat of the proconsul of Achaia, Corinth was a mini-Rome.
3. *Cultural Diversity.* Prosperity returned to the new Corinth almost immediately after it was rebuilt, attracting many people from both East and West. However, the Romans were dominant.
4. *Religious Diversity.* The Romans brought with them their culture and religions. Since Corinth was traditionally Greek, it maintained many ties with Greek religion, philosophy, and the arts. The mystery cults were brought from Egypt and Asia in the East, while the Jews worshiped in their synagogues and continued their unique belief in one God.

CORINTH: A CITY OF RELIGION AND VICE

The city of Corinth was famous in two areas: for its culture, trade, and wealth, and for its wickedness. Corinth was one of the least likely places for church planting. Religion, it has been noted, was as diverse as Corinth's population. There were as many as twenty-six sacred places devoted to the "many gods"—that is, the Greco-Roman pantheon—and "many lords"—the mystery cults (cf. 1 Cor 8:3)—and the center of worship was Aphrodite, the goddess of love, to whom many immoral priestesses were consecrated.

The city became a byword for its moral corruption, synonymous with immorality. To live like a Corinthian meant to have extremely low moral standards and loose conduct. The city was so morally perverse that its name was finally given to describe a immoral, perverted lifestyle. The good news is that, as bad as Corinth was, God had a church there. Many modern cities do not fare better than Corinth and, oftentimes, ministers find themselves facing the same challenges that confronted Paul and his converts. Believers should take heart in knowing that God is as much concerned about the cities today as was he was for the people of Corinth.

THE CHRISTIAN COMMUNITY: ETHNIC AND SOCIAL DIVERSITY

Based on the facts from Acts, 1 Corinthians, and Romans, the Corinthian community was in many ways a reflection of the city (Acts 18:1–8; 1 Cor 1:10–17; 16:15–17; Rom 16:23). It was an ethnically and socially diverse community comprising of Jews, gentiles, slaves, and free men (1 Cor 1:28–30; 12:13). There were, of course, wealthy people in the community. But according to 1:26, not many citizens came from the upper strata of society, and 7:20–24 suggests that some were slaves. Some of the tensions in the community were between the rich and the poor (1 Cor 11:17–34). Although there were some Jews in the community (Acts 18:6), passages such as 1 Corinthians 6:10–11, 8:7, and 12:2 clearly indicate that the community was primarily gentile. 1 Corinthians was primarily written to readers with a pagan past, who were once "led astray by dumb idols " (1 Cor 12:2; cf. 8:1—10:22) and needed a reminder to avoid typically pagan sexual vices (6:9–20). The same is implied in the discussion about litigation before gentile magistrates in 1 Corinthians 6:1–11 and the attitude towards marriage in 1 Corinthians 7, issues that were naturally at odds with the Judaism of the day.

WHY DID PAUL WRITE 1 CORINTHIANS?

As commonly agreed, 1 Corinthians is an occasional letter—that is, a real letter to a real people facing real problems that developed between the time Paul left the city at the end of an eighteen-month stay (cf. Acts 18) and the time of the writing of the letter, approximately three years later. Paul wrote 1 Corinthians due to three major factors. First, it was a response to reports from Chloe's household about divisions, as well other reports about sexual immorality (1 Cor 1:11; 5:1; 11:18), and to a letter sent by the Corinthians (1 Cor 7:1). Second, it was written in response to a delegation sent from Corinth to Paul (1 Cor 16). The letter shows that Paul addressed different, somewhat disparate issues, all of which (with the exception of 1 Corinthians 15) are behavioral. Even in the case of the latter, Paul's discussion on the resurrection is interspersed with ethical warnings and imperatives (1 Cor 15:33–34, 58).

MAJOR THEMES IN 1 CORINTHIANS

1. *Divisions.* The presence of internal divisions within the Corinthian congregation is clear as one reads 1 Corinthians 1:10–12, 3:4–5, and 11:18–19. The division appears to be along socioeconomic lines as shown by Paul's response in 1 Corinthians 11:17–34 (see also 1 Cor 1:26; 7:20–24; 12:13). Perhaps at the core of the problems that plagued the Corinthian Church is how members should relate to one another. There was much selfishness and individualism. Moreover, the members of the Corinthian Church were divided because they were pledging their loyalty to human leaders rather than God. It is against the backdrop of internal dissension within the Christian community at Corinth that Paul introduces the imagery of the church as a building and a temple.

2. *Holy Living.* There were serious ethical problems in this church. A Hellenistic worldview and attitude toward moral behavior considerably influenced their Christian faith. They were the Christian community in Corinth, but in many things, their attitude was more determined by their social location than by their Christian faith. It was not too long until the Corinthian Church bore the marks of the surrounding Corinthian lifestyle they had known before their conversion. They began to mirror the city where it was located. An old saint once said of the Corinthian Church, "I looked for the church and I found it in the world; and I looked for the world and I found it in the church." The temptation to conform to the surrounding culture seemed irresistible. They began to resemble and assimilate the city in which they lived, and all the sins that went along with it.

3. *Christian Freedom.* What is Christian freedom, and how should it manifest itself in daily living? Answers to these questions propel Paul's handling of food sacrificed unto idols (chapters 8–10). Located in a pluralistic society, the Corinthians were faced with problems of how to relate to those who were of opposite convictions, particularly with regards to issues of idolatrous food.

4. *Theological/Doctrinal Issues.* Several theological issues stand out in 1 Corinthians and are related to the daily living of Christians, as well as to the corporate testimony of the worshiping church. The practical problem of whether a Christian should marry and how he should conduct himself in a married or unmarried state is adequately discussed.

There were problems concerning the place of women, abuse of the Lord's Supper, and wrong use of spiritual gifts. There are several doctrinal issues interspersed within the whole book. What is the role of women in the assembly? How about the exercise of spiritual gifts? Paul also addressed the interconnected problems of church discipline and restoration.

5. *Wisdom.* One of the main misconceptions that Paul addresses in the book is wisdom. It is evident from chapters 1–4 that the Corinthians understood salvation primarily in terms of wisdom. They failed to understand the radical difference between the wisdom of the world and God's world. For the Corinthians, oratorical ability and philosophical reasoning were the measures of wisdom. For Paul, God's wisdom is not about persusavive ability, but consists of God's plan of salvation through a crucified Savior, a wisdom

6. *The Cross.* The cross of Christ is at the very heart of Paul's message and ministry at Corinth. It functioned in a polyvalent manner—that is, Paul uses it to convey meaning at several levels of perception and experience. Paul understood the cross as the unique means of God's saving grace and activity. By means of the cross, God has shown his wisdom and power in this world (1:18–24). Paul considered God's message about Christ and the cross to be more important than anything else (2:2). It is essential for Christians to constantly remember Christ's death on the cross (11:23–26). In 1 Corinthians, we find a divergence between Paul's theology of the cross and the Corinthians' theology of glory.

7. *Resurrection.* For Paul, the resurrection of Jesus from the dead is absolutely crucial to the faith. Our Christian lives are the best proof of the resurrection. First Corinthians teaches us about the resurrection of God's people. Chapter 15 is the most detailed exposition of resurrection in the New Testament. The resurrection of Jesus is tied to the resurrection of believers—that is, a future time when their bodies will become alive again. However, God has a plan to bring a new kind of life to their bodies. This will happen when Christ returns to rule (15:23–26, 51–52). Then, God will change them completely; they will never again know weakness, shame or death (15:42–43). That is the final defeat of death (15:54–57).

8. *The Holy Spirit.* It goes without saying that the church would be greatly impoverished concerning the Holy Spirit and his activities without Paul's discussion of the topic in 1 Corinthians. Paul discusses the crucial role of the Holy Spirit in every aspect of the believing community, particularly in worship and Christian formation. Paul contrasts the demonstration of the power of the Holy Spirit in the preaching of the gospel with human wisdom. In his references to the Holy Spirit indwelling the "temple" in both chapters 3 and 6, Paul unequivocally emphasizes the necessity for purity and sanctity both collectively and individually. For Paul, character and charismata must be together, not one without the other.

9. *Community.* Paul's understanding of the new community of believers is not in any way tangential to his proclamation of the gospel. Rather, it is part and parcel of that proclamation. For Paul, the church as a whole is the locus of God's eschatological activity in the interval between the resurrection and the coming of Christ. God is at work through the Spirit to create communities that prefigure and embody the reconciliation and healing of the world. The fruit of God's love is the formation of communities that confess, worship, and pray together in a way that glorifies God (see, e.g., Rom 15:7–13). Such communities are palpable signs of God's reconciliation of the world. There is a link between ecclesiology and ethics. It is not difficult to know the ethics of an individual when we know the congregation to whom one belongs. God works through the body and, as such, Paul talks about its importance. This informs Paul's use of different metaphors such as the body, temple, building, and family, among others, for the community of believers. Inseparably connected with Paul's understanding of the nature of the church is the idea of corporate responsibility. This is the notion of how the behavior of one affects the many. For Paul, there is no private sin. It may be committed privately, but it affects all. First Corinthains 5 speaks about a man having sexual relations with his father's wife, and the church kept silent, continuing to worship. Paul does not address the single person, but the whole congregation.

10. *Church Discipline.* One of the least discussed issues among Christians is church discipline. Yet, one may say that one of the most important and explicit passages on church discipline in the New Testament, and particularly in the letters of Paul, is found in 1 Corinthians 5:1–13, where he discusses the problem of an incestuous brother. Paul makes

it clear that the community mediates the demands of the gospel and its reflection on the life of the group, urging the Corinthians to take appropriate disciplinary measures. Discipline preserves the integrity of the church. Therefore, the church bears the responsibility of maintaining holiness within the body. Judgment and discipline come from the community, and so does forgiveness.

1 Corinthians 1:1–31

The Cross: God's Means of Salvation

PAUL'S APOSTOLIC GREETINGS (1:1–3)

Paul, called *as* an apostle of Jesus Christ by the will of God, and Sosthenes our brother,

2 To the church of God which is at Corinth, to those who have been sanctified in Christ Jesus, saints by calling, with all who in every place call on the name of our Lord Jesus Christ, their *Lord* and ours:

3 Grace to you and peace from God our Father and the Lord Jesus Christ.

PAUL BEGINS THE LETTER in the same form as ancient letters. He introduces himself to the addressees and greets them. There are three important things that Paul says of himself. First, he is called by God. This is an aspect of Paul's life that he stresses in his letters to the Corinthians. Paul's apostolic authority was constantly questioned by some people in Corinth. As such, the introduction is a part of his strategy to correct the misgivings that the Corinthians had about him. For Paul, his call was a divine appointment. He is an apostle through the will of God, not by human election or selection. An African proverb says that "You need only be afraid of the person who sent you on an errand, and not the person to whom you are sent." Similarly, Paul's ultimate accountability was to God. Even when things did not seem to go his way, Paul could count on the assurance that he was in the will of God.

Second, Paul's apostolic call is specific. He is called to be an apostle— that is, an emissary of Jesus Christ. Although Paul would later say that he became all things to all men in order that he might win some, there was no mistake in his mind as to who he was called to be and what he was called to do. Unlike today, when people are often described in terms of what they do (such as teaching, sewing, preaching, etc.) rather than who they are, it is significant to note that Paul's emphasis was not on doing something. Instead, he was called to be. His ministry derived from his being—that is, who he was. What a great difference that makes in one's attitude to life and ministry.

Third, Paul identifies himself with other believers. Although an apostle, Paul describes himself as a brother along with Sosthenes, of whom much is not known. Paul considered himself *as one among equals*. This ought to serve as a great lesson on humility for those who are in a position of privilege and authority.

In verse 2, the addressees are referred to as "the church of God that is in Corinth." Two things are to be noted. First, the members of the Corinthian congregation belong to God and, as such, should behave responsibly. Not only that, church leaders should act appropriately. Second is the location of the church, Corinth. Paul writes to a holy people in an unholy environment. Quite often, we hear about the universal church, but there is less emphasis placed on its geographical location. He also addresses the letter to "those who are sanctified in Christ Jesus, called to be saints." By referring to the believers as saints, Paul does not only have in mind their status as the people of God, but also the ethical obligations that follow their relationship, "with all those who in every place call on the name of our Lord Jesus Christ, both their Lord and ours." The letter was not meant for the Corinthians alone, but also for all believers in all places.

Paul then wishes the Corinthians grace and peace (v. 3). Grace has to do with both the favor that God bestowed upon the Corinthians at salvation and the continuing power to sustain their Christian life. Peace is the result of the believer's relationship with God. Peace does not necessarily imply the absence of trouble, but the calmness and assurance that derive from the knowledge that God is always in "control," no matter what. He is in charge.

PAUL'S THANKSGIVING (1:4–9)

> 4 I thank my God always concerning you for the grace of God which was given you in Christ Jesus,

> 5 that in everything you were enriched in Him, in all speech and all knowledge,
>
> 6 even as the testimony concerning Christ was confirmed in you,
>
> 7 so that you are not lacking in any gift, awaiting eagerly the revelation of our Lord Jesus Christ,
>
> 8 who will also confirm you to the end, blameless in the day of our Lord Jesus Christ.
>
> 9 God is faithful, through whom you were called into fellowship with His Son, Jesus Christ our Lord.

Paul gives thanks to God on behalf of the Corinthians for various reasons. First, he gives thanks to God for the grace of God that was bestowed upon them. In emphasizing God's grace, from the onset Paul made the important point that whatever they had or were was due to God's grace. Second, the Corinthians were enriched in everything by God. There seems to be a play on words by Paul as "grace" (*charis*, v. 5) and "gift" (*charismata*, v. 7) both derive from the same root. In today's world, there seems to be more emphasis on charisma than character and on gifts than grace. For Paul, the one presumes the other. Character and grace should be at the foundation of charisma and gifts. The Corinthians need to know that. So do we.

Third, Paul gives thanks to God that the Corinthians had been spiritually enriched by God, and goes on to say that the testimony of Christ was confirmed among them (in you), not just individually, but corporately. Paul's gospel is here called the "testimony" of Christ. The Corinthians, whose lives have been transformed in a dramatic fashion, are the demonstration of the power of the gospel of God's grace. In the same manner that the gospel was confirmed among the Corinthians, they would be confirmed by God in the end when Christ appears. Paul ends the section with a powerful truth: God is faithful.

QUARRELS AND DIVISIONS (1:10–17)

> 10 Now I exhort you, brethren, by the name of our Lord Jesus Christ, that you all agree and that there be no divisions among you, but that you be made complete in the same mind and in the same judgment.
>
> 11 For I have been informed concerning you, my brethren, by Chloe's *people*, that there are quarrels among you.

> 12 Now I mean this, that each one of you is saying, "I am of Paul," and "I of Apollos," and "I of Cephas," and "I of Christ."
>
> 13 Has Christ been divided? Paul was not crucified for you, was he? Or were you baptized in the name of Paul?
>
> 14 I thank God that I baptized none of you except Crispus and Gaius,
>
> 15 so that no one would say you were baptized in my name.
>
> 16 Now I did baptize also the household of Stephanas; beyond that, I do not know whether I baptized any other.
>
> 17 For Christ did not send me to baptize, but to preach the gospel, not in cleverness of speech, so that the cross of Christ would not be made void.

Having concluded the introduction to the letter, Paul comes to the main point that he is about to address in the first four chapters of the epistle, an exhortation for the Corinthians to put an end to all squabbles. Verse 10 is an appeal (Paul starts with "now I plead with you") for a common mind and the repudiation of cliques. In this first verse of the body of the letter, Paul calls the Corinthian believers to perfect Christian unity. The word "appeal" carries with it the connotations of request and exhortation. The basis of Paul's appeal is striking. He does not make his appeal on the basis of his apostolic authority. Instead, Paul first appeals to the Corinthians as "brethren" (brothers and sisters), a word that is not only familial, but also connotes equality. He stands on common ground with those to whom he wrote.

Second, he appeals to them on account of the name of the Lord Jesus Christ. The intensity of his feelings is immediately revealed as he solemnly appeals to them in the name of the Lord Jesus. As Chrysostom says, "he nails them to his name." Paul's appeal is for the Corinthians to do away with all "divisions," literally "schisms" (Greek *schismata*), a metaphor related to clothing. Thus, what Paul is saying is that there be no ripping apart in the community. Rather, as one piece of cloth, the people of God should be perfectly united. In turn, such unity is to be evidenced in their confession—they were to speak the same thing. To be united in the same mind is to share the same convictions about God and Jesus Christ. Paul tells them to speak the same thing and exhorts them to avoid ministry–based factions. It is possible to have different views and not be divisive.

The reason for the appeal is provided in 1 Corinthians 3:3, where Paul states that if the Christians are divided they are no different from other people. In that case, it is impossible for them to do the special work to which God has called them. So deep is Paul's concern for the Corinthians that he reiterates his plea for unity three times over in this verse: that all of you be in agreement and there be no divisions among you, but that you be united in the same mind and the same purpose.

Verses 11–12 show the reason why Paul considers the plea so urgently necessary. Paul has received a report from Chloe's people. The fact that there were contentions among them was something that was made explicitly clear to Paul and was beyond dispute; therefore, he could confidently address the situation. Paul's method is equally instructive. He did not hide the identity of Chloe, and just refers to her report as an "anonymous report." The gravity of the divisions is shown in the use of the word "contention" (Greek *eris*). In its original usage, it always referred to disputes that endanger the church. The word points to quarrels and is the hot dispute, the emotional flame that ignites whenever rivalry becomes intolerable. It is listed as one of the works of the flesh in Galatians 5:20 of which Christians should have no part.

In verse 12, Paul becomes more specific as he writes about the content of the report that he received. The mistake which the Corinthians were making was to put a human leader in the place of God. What a tragedy, and how true it is, even in the twenty-first century. Apparently, the members of the Corinthian Church were divisively forming particular allegiances to various leaders within themselves. The exact nature of the divisions in the church cannot be fully determined, other than that they were drawn along partisan lines. Each group in the congregation used the name of a particular leader—Paul, Peter, Apollos, and even Jesus—as a "war cry." Most of them gave their loyalties to human leaders instead of Jesus Christ. Somehow, as they magnified the human instruments, they had lost sight of the Savior. It is a mistake Christians and others have often made and continue to make. There are still many groups and religious organizations that honor one human being, particularly the founder, as if he/she were a sort of second Christ. But Paul would have none of it. One group in the Corinthian Church prided itself in belonging to Christ. However, they were wrong in claiming an exclusive relationship with Christ that others either did not have or could not obtain. So Paul said that Jesus is for everyone. Therefore, no Christians have the right to think that Jesus belongs to their groups, religious and denominational affiliations, in an exclusive manner. Divisions, schisms, and factions belong to the old self.

Paul asks three rhetorical questions that underline the irrationality of the state of affairs in the Corinthian Church that he has just sketched in verse 13. The answer to each question is an unequivocal no. "Has Christ been divided?" Inherent in this question is the idea of the church as the body of Christ, which Paul would later develop in 1 Corinthians 10–12. Christ cannot be divided, for he is one (1 Cor 12:12), nor can he be apportioned out so that only one group may claim to follow him. Rather, all of the Corinthians are supposed to follow Christ. "Paul was not crucified for you, was he?" Paul was not, nor were they baptized into his name. Only to the extent that Paul follows and imitates Christ were the Corinthians to follow and imitate Paul (1 Cor 11:1). The point is, the Corinthians were in danger of giving to mere human leaders that ultimate allegiance which belongs to Christ alone, as their only Savior. As Paul will put it in 4:1, the Corinthians should think of Paul and his fellow apostles simply as servants of Christ, to whom the mysteries of God are committed and who are responsible to him. Paul continues with another question: "Or were you baptized in the name of Paul?" Some Corinthians were probably flaunting the name of the person who baptized them, suggesting that such persons were either more spiritual or exhibited greater wisdom. Once again, Paul uses his own name to demonstrate the error of the Corinthian partisanship. The phrase "in the name," literally "into the name" when used with baptism, implies that the subject is baptized the exclusive property of Christ.

Was Paul saying that baptism was unnecessary in verses 14–17? Absolutely not. One should by no means interpret or understand these verses as such. Paul simply placed the proper emphasis where it belongs—that is, the preaching of the gospel (see v. 17). Nevertheless, when Paul was with the Corinthians, as far as he could possibly recall, he only baptized a few people, something which he might have considered providential, for if Paul had indeed baptized many of them, they could have used that to support the absurdity of the claims found in verses 12–13. Paul can say with certainty that he baptized Crispus, the synagogue ruler (Acts 18:8); Gaius, his host (Rom 16:23); and the household of Stephanas (cf. 1 Cor 16:15–16).

If baptism is not Paul's primary task, what is? Paul here reiterates his God-given commission. It was "to preach the gospel." Had the Corinthians recognized the meaning or import of their baptism, they would know that they had been baptized into Christ, not into any human being. Baptism was not insignificant to Paul, as Romans 6:3–7 shows. However, it was secondary to the proclamation of the gospel, for which Christ sent Paul. The word "sent" (Greek *apeistelein*) is the verb form of the noun "apostle," which indicates the special task to which Paul was called, as well as the source of authority by which he carried out the task. Paul's authority derives from

The Cross: God's Means of Salvation

God and lies in being Christ's apostle, Christ's "sent one." As for the manner in which his task is to be carried out, it is imperative that this is consistent with the content of his message, which is the good news of God's saving work in Christ. As such, Paul's gospel proclamation is not to be done with humanistic rhetorical eloquence or worldly wisdom, which would render the cross of Christ powerless. For Paul, there can be no room for pyrotechnic displays of rhetorical brilliance such as were offered by the traveling sophists, whose voices were often heard in the marketplaces on any Mediterranean city. Such a method of proclamation would only serve to exalt the proclaimer and not the One proclaimed. If Paul had done so, then he could have been guilty of promoting the factions spoken of in verses 11–13. But, on the contrary, Paul promoted true Christian unity through his undiluted proclamation of Christ crucified. The unified speaking, mind, and judgment that the Corinthian believers are called to have in verse 10 are to originate from, and be centered on, the message of the cross of Christ which Paul proclaims. In this verse, Paul lays the groundwork for what he will immediately say about his evangelizing (1:18—2:5).

THE MESSAGE OF THE CROSS VERSUS HUMAN WISDOM (1:18–25)

> 18 For the word of the cross is foolishness to those who are perishing, but to us who are being saved it is the power of God.
>
> 19 For it is written, "I will destroy the wisdom of the wise, And the cleverness of the clever I will set aside."
>
> 20 Where is the wise man? Where is the scribe? Where is the debater of this age? Has not God made foolish the wisdom of the world?
>
> 21 For since in the wisdom of God the world through its wisdom did not *come to* know God, God was well-pleased through the foolishness of the message preached to save those who believe.
>
> 22 For indeed Jews ask for signs and Greeks search for wisdom;
>
> 23 but we preach Christ crucified, to Jews a stumbling block and to Gentiles foolishness,
>
> 24 but to those who are the called, both Jews and Greeks, Christ the power of God and the wisdom of God.
>
> 25 Because the foolishness of God is wiser than men, and the weakness of God is stronger than men.

In the immediately preceding section (1:10–17), Paul had appealed for unity in the church. He now moves on a different argumentative tack, launching into an extended discussion in which, on the one hand, he elucidates the significance and meaning of the cross and, on the other hand, shows that the prideful confidence of the Corinthians on human wisdom is contrary to the gospel. The basic theme of this section of the letter is the opposition between human/worldly wisdom and the "word of the cross" or "God's wisdom."

In verses 18–25, Paul shows the incompatibility of the cross and human wisdom. To some of the Corinthians, as well as it is to others today, a crucified Savior is a contradiction in terms. It is in fact perceived as "foolishness" (v. 18). To associate weakness with Christ who is the Deliverer made no sense both to the Greeks and Jews. Not so for Paul and the Corinthian believers whose lives have been changed by the gospel message. To those who are perishing, the message of the cross is foolishness, but to those who are being saved, it is the power of God. Ultimately, for Paul, it is one's response to the cross that determines one's eternal destiny. The person who rejects the cross is on the road to eternal death, whereas the one who embraces it is, wherein the power of God is displayed, assured of eternal salvation. Note that Paul spoke of only two classes of people: the perishing and the saved. All of humanity falls into one of these two classes. What a sharp contrast to the way people are classified or categorized today. In today's world, people are categorized based on which part of the world they come from, the color of their skin, their level of education, and whether they are male or female. Such classifications are of no value to God. One is either lost in sin, a child of Satan, or saved by grace through faith in the atoning work of Christ on Calvary. Paul quotes Isaiah 29:14 and 33:18 in order to show both the limitation and futility of human wisdom (v. 19). The four rhetorical questions in verse 20 and the statements that follow in verses 21–25 further affirm Paul's claim that human wisdom as demonstrated by the Jews for signs and the quest of the Greeks for wisdom is of no use with regards to the salvation of humankind. The concepts of sin, guilt, and atonement were totally foreign and repugnant to Greek philosophy. They really failed to understand what was going on in the world. Therefore, there was no need for the cross. But for Paul, Christ's crucifixion is the crux of his message and his own understanding of God's matchless wisdom. As Isaiah said, God's ways are not our ways, and his thoughts are higher than human thoughts. Paul's fundamental theological point is that if the cross is God's saving event, all human standards and evaluation are overturned. Instead of being instruments of salvation, the signs demanded by the Jews and the wisdom sought after by them are stumbling blocks and foolishness respectively.

GOD'S WISDOM VERSUS HUMAN FOOLISHNESS (1:26–31)

> 26 For consider your calling, brethren, that there were not many wise according to the flesh, not many mighty, not many noble;
> 27 but God has chosen the foolish things of the world to shame the wise, and God has chosen the weak things of the world to shame the things which are strong,
> 28 and the base things of the world and the despised God has chosen, the things that are not, so that He may nullify the things that are,
> 29 so that no man may boast before God.
> 30 But by His doing you are in Christ Jesus, who became to us wisdom from God, and righteousness and sanctification, and redemption,
> 31 so that, just as it is written, "Let him who boasts, boast in the Lord."

To further bolster his claim that God's wisdom surpasses human folly, Paul appealed to the social location of the Corinthians. The thought of the contradiction of God's method to human wisdom is illustrated by the kind of people that he has called. Although the Corinthian Church must have been comprised of people from different walks of life, including some rich and knowledgeable people, Paul says that many of them were indeed poor and not "schooled" (vv. 27–28). Yet, it is to those people who are regarded as foolish and weak that God has demonstrated his power as they embraced the message of the cross. God does not show favoritism to people because of what they have, what they know, who they are, and where they come from. All are equal before him and saved the same way. Therefore, no flesh may glory in his presence (v. 29). Paul presents the benefits of Christ to the Corinthians in particular, and to all believers at large, in a fourfold but necessarily sequential manner (v. 30). First, he is the true wisdom of God, as opposed to the human wisdom that the Greeks boasted of. Second, Christ is the believers' righteousness. How true are Augustus M. Toplady's words: "In my hand, no price I bring, simply to the Cross I cling." Third, Christ is the believers' sanctification. The holiness of believers is grounded both on the work of Christ and their relationship with him. Fourth, Christ is the believers' redemption. The word "redemption," as used here, seems to summarize all that Paul has just said. Christ paid it all. Hence, Paul concludes, "He who glories, let him glory in the Lord" (v. 31). Thus, believers need to be cautioned to avoid any reliance on worldly wisdom. Jessie B. Pounds (1906) captured the heart of Paul's teaching when he wrote the great hymn "The Way of the Cross Leads Home":

> I must needs go home by the way of the cross,
> There's no other way but this;
> I shall ne'er get sight of the gates of light
> If the way of the cross I miss.
>
> Refrain
> The way of the cross leads home,
> The way of the cross leads home,
> It is sweet to know as I onward go,
> The way of the cross leads home.
>
> I must needs go on in the blood-sprinkled way,
> The path that the Savior trod,
> If I ever climb to the heights sublime,
> Where the soul is at home with God.
>
> Then I bid farewell to the way of the world,
> To walk in it never more;
> For the Lord says, "Come," and I seek my home,
> Where He waits at the open door.

QUESTIONS FOR PERSONAL REFLECTION

1. How important is the issue of unity in the church today? In what way can members contribute to the unity of the church both locally and on a larger level?

2. What is the relationship between a person's calling and mission? How significant is it for one to be sure of his or her calling?

3. At such a time when there is much emphasis on "wealth and wonders," how can the church recapture the preaching of the crucified Christ? What are the likely results of such proclamation?
4. To what extent is my faith in Christ bound up in a particular messenger or minister?
5. Do I think more as an individual, or as a person whose significance is bound up in the membership of the body of Christ?
6. Usually, authority and humility do not go together. How did Paul manage to successfully hold both together?

1 Corinthians 2:1–16

Human Wisdom versus God's Wisdom

THE STORY IS TOLD of the Moravians, a people committed to Jesus Christ and moved of God to take the gospel right across the world to Greenland. When they were beginning their mission there, they found that the natives were so ignorant that they were at the end of their tether as to how to share the gospel with them. Because the natives could not understand the language of the missionaries, and could neither read nor write, the missionaries decided that they would first and foremost teach them how to read and write. The attempt was a dismal failure.

While one of the missionaries was awaiting a ship to take him home, he began to translate a portion of the Gospels in the New Testament. After he had finished translating that portion, he decided that he would test the translation by opening the word of God and reading it to the native people. As he did that, he read to them about the death, the crucifixion, the cross of our Lord Jesus Christ. After finishing reading the portion of Scripture in their own native tongue, there was a pause, after which the head of the tribe stood up and asked that the missionary would read the portion of the gospel again. After he finished reading it, the chief said, "Is what you read true? Is it true?" The missionary replied, saying "It is true." In response, the chief proclaimed, "Then why didn't you tell us this at first? Why did you have to leave it until now? We will listen now to the words of this Man who suffered for us! You cannot go, you will have to stay and tell us about this suffering Man who suffered for us!" This story illustrates the point of this chapter, that a simple proclamation of the gospel always conquers where human wisdom fails. The cross trumps human wisdom!

HUMAN WISDOM VERSUS GOD'S WISDOM

PAUL'S DEPENDENCE ON THE HOLY SPIRIT'S POWER (2:1–5)

> 1 And when I came to you, brethren, I did not come with superiority of speech or of wisdom, proclaiming to you the testimony of God.
>
> 2 For I determined to know nothing among you except Jesus Christ, and Him crucified.
>
> 3 I was with you in weakness and in fear and in much trembling,
>
> 4 and my message and my preaching were not in persuasive words of wisdom, but in demonstration of the Spirit and of power,
>
> 5 so that your faith would not rest on the wisdom of men, but on the power of God.

Paul continues to address the problem of "wisdom" preaching in Corinth. As we saw in the previous chapter, some people were placing undue emphasis on the wisdom of the Greeks. They liked to make impressive speeches to show off their wisdom. Paul must have been a great disappointment to the philosophers of Corinth when they first heard him. He was a learned person, but did not try to impress them with clever speaking. He presented the gospel in simple words, using himself as an illustration of the difference between divine and human wisdom. The conversion of the Corinthians was a testimony to the power of God, and not the persuasion of logic.

In verse 1, Paul alludes to his visit to Corinth (cf. Acts 18:1–18) when the Corinthians first heard the message and believed. He reminded the Corinthians of "when I came to you," Most of the Corinthians surely remembered the time. But how did Paul come? Did he move the people with outstanding oratory and concise logic? Not at all! So, Paul contrasts himself with some other preachers by using a Greek word which means, "*I* for *my* part (as opposed to others)." He maintains that his message was simple. He refused to take any credit as an orator. He did not compete with his opponents, who used their clever speeches to impress the worldly wise Corinthians. To do so would empty the cross of its power. He sought to remind the Corinthians that his own preaching to them had conformed to what he has said about the "foolishness" of the gospel. Paul restates what he previously said in 1:17. It was not his own clever preaching or oratorical skill which led the Corinthians to believe in Jesus Christ. It was the experience of the power of God's spirit as shown by Paul that impressed them as he explained the mystery of God. Paul could easily have credited his success to his own oratorical skill, hard work, or intellect. But to do so would have negated his own admonition at the conclusion of chapter 1, where he cites Jeremiah 9:24: "Let him who boasts, boast in the Lord." He begins by doing exactly that. Paul shows an example that he lives what he preaches.

Paul's example provides a useful lesson for preachers today. Think of preachers you hear. Do they like to show off, use fancy words and clever techniques? Is their delivery more important to them than their content? Or do they speak simply and explain things clearly? But Paul chose a simple delivery of a powerful message. This is not to say that he was muddled or badly prepared. Rather, his message was always given greater importance than his method of delivering it. Concerning wisdom, Paul could be regarded as a scholar of the highest order, but he never sought to display his scholarship when preaching. Good preaching does not consist of words that draw attention to the preacher's personal attainments or cleverness of voice, but words that point to the presence and activity of God. It does not express what the hearers love to hear, but inspires the hearers to turn to God. The mystery of God is the message that the Corinthians did not understand before, It is here explained by Paul and illuminated by the Holy Spirit (2:10-14). The mystery that Paul preached relates to Christ and the cross. As Paul showed earlier, both the Jews and Greeks had no clue concerning the significance of the cross.

In verse 2, Paul stated his normal practice. He was only concerned with what he considered as the central truths of the gospel: Christ and his crucifixion. It was the power of God through the gospel of Christ that changed the Corinthians. So, there was no reason for Paul to change his focus. Paul goes on to further describe the manner of his coming (v. 3). While on the one hand Paul preached with fear and trembling, on the other hand, he preached with the power of the Holy Spirit. Here is a contrast between Paul's human weakness and the power of the gospel supported by the Holy Spirit. Paul describes his presence with the Corinthians being "in weakness, fear, and trembling." He did not come to Corinth in his own strength and power. Although other passages in the New Testament alert us to weaknesses of Paul (Gal 4:14; 6:10; 2 Cor 12:7-10), it is unlikely that Paul was referring to physical weakness here. Rather, Paul was referring to his utter helplessness in convincing his hearers with ordinary human persuasive ability. Unlike some other preachers in the Corinthian congregation, Paul did not attempt to use "enticing words," nor did he attempt to speak human wisdom. Paul's preaching was not validated by eloquence and sophistication, but with demonstrations of the Spirit's power. The term used for demonstration carries a legal sense of irrefutable proof. The Corinthians must place their faith in the work of the Spirit, rather than human wisdom.

With regards to presentation, Paul affirms not only that the content of his preaching had been purely and simply the wisdom of God, but also that the manner of his presentation had also been entirely consistent with his theme. He did not depend on plausible or persuasive words of human wisdom—that is, overpowering oratory or philosophical argument or human wisdom. Paul had come to them without any pretensions to eloquence or wisdom in declaring the truth about God (v. 4). The faith of the Corinthians must rest in God rather than human persuasiveness (v. 5). The apostles were not learned, yet they were effective. Christian history is replete with men and women such as Dwight L. Moody, Mary Slessor, John Bunyan, Smith Wigglesworth, Billy Bray, Joseph Babalola of Nigeria, and others who, despite lack of great pedigree or extraordinary academic achievements, were effective preachers and missionaries who led many people to Christ.

GOD'S WISDOM (2:6–16)

> 6 Yet we do speak wisdom among those who are mature; a wisdom, however, not of this age nor of the rulers of this age, who are passing away;
>
> 7 but we speak God's wisdom in a mystery, the hidden *wisdom* which God predestined before the ages to our glory;
>
> 8 *the wisdom* which none of the rulers of this age has understood; for if they had understood it they would not have crucified the Lord of glory;
>
> 9 but just as it is written, "Things which eye has not seen and ear has not heard,
>
> And *which* have not entered the heart of man, All that God has prepared for those who love Him."
>
> 10 For to us God revealed *them* through the Spirit; for the Spirit searches all things, even the depths of God.
>
> 11 For who among men knows the *thoughts* of a man except the spirit of the man which is in him? Even so the *thoughts* of God no one knows except the Spirit of God.
>
> 12 Now we have received, not the spirit of the world, but the Spirit who is from God, so that we may know the things freely given to us by God,

> 13 which things we also speak, not in words taught by human wisdom, but in those taught by the Spirit, combining spiritual *thoughts* with spiritual *words*.
>
> 14 But a natural man does not accept the things of the Spirit of God, for they are foolishness to him; and he cannot understand them, because they are spiritually appraised.
>
> 15 But he who is spiritual appraises all things, yet he himself is appraised by no one.
>
> 16 For who has known the mind of the Lord, that he will instruct Him? But we have the mind of Christ.

Lest some Corinthians come to the wrong conclusion that the gospel is devoid of wisdom (v. 16), Paul states that he speaks wisdom, but it is only intelligible to "those who are mature" (v. 6). "Mature" here refers to the saved—those enlightened by the Holy Spirit—in contrast with the unsaved. Paul insists that his teaching is not the product of human intellectual activity; it is the gift of God, and it came into the world with Jesus Christ. This wisdom, Paul says, does not come from this age of time and space, and certainly not from the rulers of this age (those who are of highest importance in the world), because such people crucified the Lord of glory (v. 8).

Paul's presentation of God's eternal plan of salvation (v. 7) is based, through the Holy Spirit, on the wisdom of God revealed to him and to others. God's wisdom is contained in a mystery, and has been planned before the beginning of the ages. God's plan of salvation is no afterthought. That plan, although revealed in the Old Testament, is not as fully explained and understood there as it is in the New Testament. Mystery does not mean something esoteric or something necessarily unknown, but something not as fully understood at one time as it was at another (see Dan 2:18–36; 4:9; Rom 16:25–26). It demands an explanation, just as Cornelius, in response to Philip's question ("Do you understand what you are reading?"), says, "How can I unless someone guides me?" (Acts 8:30–31). The secular and religious rulers (Acts 4:25–28) of Jesus' days revealed their ignorance through the way they treated him. Had they understood, they would not have crucified the Lord of glory (v. 8). Christ's divinity and his human nature are now brought together by the apostle. He concludes that God the Son, as incarnate in man, died on the cross. Paul signals his intention to refer to the Old Testament by saying "it is written." He loosely quotes Isaiah 64:4. The "hidden wisdom" he has been preaching is the wisdom referred to in the Old Testament—it was set forth on the promises God had prepared and laid up for those who love him. It is these promises that people like the

Human Wisdom versus God's Wisdom

rulers of this world do not see and have not obeyed. The thought of them has not even entered the natural man's mind. In saving his people by means of the gospel, God surpasses their expectation and does for them things unheard before—things which no eye has seen, nor ear heard, nor the human heart conceived. But to Paul, to the other apostles, and their fellow workers, in contrast to the unsaved rulers of the world, God revealed them through the Spirit (v. 10). The Greek verb Paul uses is also used in Matthew 16:17 and Luke 10:22 to indicate divine revelation of certain supernatural secrets. It is also used in an eschatological sense of the revelation connected with certain persons and events (Rom 8:18; 1 Cor 3:13) for the Spirit reveals everything, even the depths of God.

Paul goes on to provide an illustration that will show that the spiritual wisdom and truths of God can be understood only through the Holy Spirit, just as human wisdom needs the human spirit to understand it. So no one truly comprehends what is truly God's except the Spirit of God: The conclusion is that only the Holy Spirit can reveal God's wisdom and truth to humankind. In contrast to some other kind of spirit, through which some might try to know God's wisdom and truth (like the spirit of the wisdom of this world [1 Cor 1:20; 2:6; 3:19]), believers have received the Spirit who is from God—as such, they can now understand and know the gifts that are bestowed on them by God.

Paul's argument in this section reminds us of the story of an incident that occurred at Boston during the Christmas season in 1879. An agnostic reporter saw three little girls standing in front of a store window full of toys. One of them was blind. He heard the other two describing the toys to their friend. He had never considered how difficult it was to explain to someone without sight what something looks like. That incident became the basis for a newspaper story. Two weeks later, the reporter attended a meeting held by Dwight L. Moody. His purpose was to catch the evangelist in an inconsistency. He was surprised when Moody used his account of the children to illustrate a truth. "Just as the blind girl couldn't visualize the toys," said Moody, "so an unsaved person can't see Christ in all His glory." Today many are unaware of the true identity of Jesus Christ and are ignorant of the saving power of the gospel. It requires the Spirit of God to illuminate a person's heart (Rom 8:9b).

In verse 13, Paul reverts to the nature of his own ministry (cf. vv. 4–5). He wants it known that he speaks "not in words taught . . . by human wisdom but in words taught by the Spirit," as he and other associates express spiritual truths in words conveying the real spiritual truth. Human nature does not accept the illumination and truths from the Spirit of God. Humans consider those truths to be foolish and, therefore, do not receive the gifts of God's Spirit, for they are foolishness to them. Paul makes it even stronger when that such person is unable to understand them (the things/gifts of God) because they are spiritually discerned. He or she cannot make spiritually intelligent decisions.

In contrast to the natural "person" in verse 14, the one who is spiritual, being guided by the Spirit, discerns all things—that is, is able to draw intelligent conclusions about all kinds of spiritual things. Paul appeals to Isaiah 40:13 at the beginning of 1 Corinthians 2:15 to reinforce the idea that no one can fully grasp the mind of God. Although the quotation, in its question form, initially appears on the possibility of knowing God's wisdom, the latter part (v. 16b) gives reassurance that the Christian does know it. This explains verse 15b—the person who has God's Spirit is not subject to judgments by one who does not have the Spirit. This directly relates to Paul's situation—the Greek philosophers and the sign-seeking Jews may mock and jeer, but they are both incapable and unqualified to judge the message of Paul and other Christians who have the mind of Christ because they do not have the Spirit of God and cannot judge spiritual truths. Unlike the Corinthians who, as a result of their so-called wisdom, were causing divisions, those who have the mind of Christ are not focused on special wisdom or experiences, but on community life. The mind of Christ is characterized by death to selfish ambitions, humbling of oneself, and giving oneself to others. Having the mind of Christ enables Christians to think about life the way that Jesus himself did, with the keen ability to observe what goes on around them and act appropriately. It engenders compassion for the less privileged and suffering, kindness for the destitute, and courage to stand up to the rich and powerful when necessary.

QUESTIONS FOR PERSONAL REFLECTION

1. Based on this chapter, how should one evaluate good or bad preaching?
2. How is the wisdom of God often seen as foolishness by humans?
3. Considering Paul's discussion in this chapter, do you consider yourself to be a mature Christian, or do you lack in spiritual discernment?

4. What is the true test of spirituality?
5. How do you understand the ministry of the Holy Spirit in revealing the deep things of God?

1 Corinthians 3:1–23

The Nature of Christian Leadership

IMAGINE AN ADULT, A grown person, who behaves like a baby! A person who has never developed, who is growing old, but not growing up! Imagine further that the lack of growth is neither genetic nor forced upon the person. Rather, it is actually an intelligent choice to remain a baby! To choose to never grow! Imagine, if you will, a fifty-year-old woman turning up for work with a bib around her neck, a pacifier in her mouth, and her favorite toy underneath her arm! What would it be like to see a sixty-five-year-old man surrounded by toys? Ridiculous, one would say. And so it is. What Paul says in this chapter is worse than these examples. The Corinthians have the power of God, the gifts of the Spirit, and the riches of grace, all at their disposal. But they willingly refused to grow and to mature. They chose to remain as babes.

BABES IN CHRIST (3:1–4)

> 1 And I, brethren, could not speak to you as to spiritual men, but as to men of flesh, as to infants in Christ.
> 2 I gave you milk to drink, not solid food; for you were not yet able *to receive it*. Indeed, even now you are not yet able,
> 3 for you are still fleshly. For since there is jealousy and strife among you, are you not fleshly, and are you not walking like mere men?
> 4 For when one says, "I am of Paul," and another, "I am of Apollos," are you not *mere* men?

The Nature of Christian Leadership

Over the years, I have heard people appeal to 1 Corinthians 3:1–3 and say "I am just a carnal Christian," primarily as a way to justify their immature decisions and actions. Such people wear their "carnality" as a badge of honor. It shows their lack of understanding of the possibility of grace and belies Paul's optimistic view of victorious Christian living. This seems to be the case with the Corinthians, whose "carnality" is displayed in various ways, particularly in the factionalization of the community along leadership lines. Paul continues to deal with the problem of divisions (vv. 4–5) that plagued the Corinthian Church. He shows that the problem lay in the Corinthians' lack of spiritual immaturity. They were babes in Christ, like children at the breast, needing to be fed with milk and not meat. They were different from mature people, described as "spiritual." As infants, the Corinthians were incapable of judging what was most suitable for themselves. They were unqualified to discern between one teacher and another. They have no right judgment, and this springs from their lack of knowledge in spiritual matters. They did not act like people who were "in the spirit" or "spiritual." Furthermore, Paul describes them as "merely human." They acted as persons under the influence of fleshly appetites. They coveted the things of this life rather than concentrating on spiritual things. Babies are usually selfish, preoccupied with themselves. Such was the state of the Corinthians. In this verse, Paul overturns the Corinthians' estimate of themselves. In order to show the extent of the immaturity of the Corinthians, Paul said that he has fed them with milk. He means that he has only instructed them in the basics of Christianity because they are too young in faith to understand the deeper truths of the gospel. The apostle shows them the absurdity of their conduct in pretending to judge between preacher and preacher, while they only had a "baby's" knowledge of the first principles of Christianity. He could not feed them with "solid food," because as infants in Christ they could not spiritually digest it.

In verse 3, Paul describes the Corinthians again as being "of the flesh." To be controlled by the flesh is to have an outlook that is orientated toward self, that which pursues its own ends in autonomy from God. They were living in a way that was sub-Christian. Paul's illustrates this self-orientation by reminding them of the "jealousy" and, "quarreling" which plague the Christian community. He hints at their divisions (v. 4). One of the reasons why Paul describes them in this manner was because they were aligning themselves with various teachers. They were dividing up into various camps: the followers of Apollos and the followers of Paul. Paul says that all of that is merely human. That is how the world looks at things. The world divides us all up in status, rank, and order. The world does that in many different ways—for example, racially, educationally, or socioeconomically. But the church doesn't operate like the world. When one is involved in jealousy, quarrels, and division, one gives evidence that he or she is still an infant, a spiritual baby. Paul states the question in a way that expects a positive answer. This suggests that the Corinthians, if they were being honest with themselves, should admit their failing here. To walk "according to human inclinations" means to live only the way the ordinary sinful person lives: in selfishness, pride, and envy. Such a walk is that which conforms to a human rather than a godly standard. Their immaturity led to contentiousness. The behavior of the Corinthians shows that they were all too human, contrary to their claim of spirituality. They were continually disputing and contending whose party was the best, each faction endeavoring to prove that it was right. Envy and grudges led to strife, and this led to divisions.

Verse 4 brings us back to the actual state of the Corinthian Christians, with their divisive preferences for individual apostles and ministers. Paul's example of himself and Apollos, who shared in the ministry at Corinth (Acts 18:1–28), was needed to show the Corinthians that they had a distorted view of the Lord's work. Whenever they thought of God's work in terms of belonging to or following a particular Christian worker, they were simply acting on the human level and taking sides just as the world does. The Corinthians were probably captivated by the outward manners of Paul and Apollos, rather than their teaching. Apollos was more eloquent than Paul. Their preferring one to another on such an account proved that they were merely human—led by their senses and mere outward appearances, without being under the guidance either of reason or grace. There are thousands of such people in the Christian Church till the present day. Some follow particular leaders because of their charisma and eloquence, while others prefer preachers that are deemed successful because of their financial prosperity. In either case, the main consideration is not the spirituality of the leaders.

PAUL AND APOLLOS AS SERVANTS (3:5–9)

> 5 What then is Apollos? And what is Paul? Servants through whom you believed, even as the Lord gave *opportunity* to each one.
> 6 I planted, Apollos watered, but God was causing the growth.

> 7 So then neither the one who plants nor the one who waters is anything, but God who causes the growth.
> 8 Now he who plants and he who waters are one; but each will receive his own reward according to his own labor.
> 9 For we are God's fellow workers; you are God's field, God's building.

Paul responds to the implicit question, "How should the Corinthians view Paul and Apollos?" He wants to impress the Corinthians with the fact that he and Apollos are simply servants, so he uses "what" instead of "who." The question becomes this: "What then is Paul, and what is Apollos?" No Christian worker is ever to be idolized. Indeed, those who are idolized can become instruments for fragmenting the work of God. Believers are to realize that Christian workers are simply God's servants—agents through whom people believe in Christ. The word *diakonoi*, from which we get "deacon," has also been translated "minister." It is properly used for attendants and waiters, those who serve others. God has not called Paul and Apollos to be masters of the Corinthian Christians. They were to serve them and meet their needs. Here again, we see the self-effacing attitude of Paul. He was the one who sowed the seed of the gospel in the region. However, he neither overestimates his own labors, nor detracts anything from the real excellence of Apollos as a workman. Instead, Paul ascribes to God the full glory, as the giver of all good. As in the natural so in the *spiritual* world, he says. It is by the special blessing of God that the grain sown in the ground brings forth thirty, sixty, or a hundredfold. It is neither the sower nor the waterer that produces this strange and inexplicable multiplication; it is God alone. God alone should have all the glory. The *seed* is his, the ground is his, the laborers are his, and all the produce comes from himself. Ministers are instruments in God's hand. They depend on God's blessing, to make their work fruitful. Without this they are nothing; their part is so small that they hardly deserve to be mentioned.

Paul goes on to make a twofold emphasis. On the one hand, Paul and Apollos, though exercising different roles, are both engaged in the one mission—both have to be commissioned to propagate the gospel. They were both meant to labor to promote the glory of God in the salvation of the souls of the Corinthians. The question, then, is this: "Why should the Corinthians be divided with respect to Paul and Apollos, while these apostles are intimately united in spirit and purpose?" Although their functions are different, nevertheless, they are united. On the other hand, each one is to be rewarded according to his labor. Each one is responsible to God. There is, therefore, no need for competition. Perhaps nowhere is this better illustrated than in Jesus' parable of the ten slaves and ten pounds (cf. Luke 19:11–26). In that parable, Jesus shows that God has called each of us. He has gifted us and equipped us for the work of ministry. And he has work for us to do. This is true for every believer in his church. None is excluded from having a place of service in his kingdom. We all have kingdom work! And whosoever is faithful to the work he or she is called to do will be accordingly rewarded. It is instructive to note that both in the parable of Jesus and Paul's discussion here, reward is not according to the measure of success. Rather, it is according to the labor of each, that is, according to faithfulness.

Paul employs two images to drive home the point that he and Apollos are simply fellow workers in God's service. First, he says that they are the field. Perhaps he brings to the minds of the Corinthians the farming going on in the plain below the city. But Paul does not stop there. He introduces another imagery, describing the Corinthians as God's building. They are not only the field which God cultivates, but they are the house which God builds, and in which he intends to dwell. Generally, when viewing a magnificent building, the praise goes not to the quarryman that dug up the stones, nor the mason that placed them in the wall, nor the carpenter that jointed it, but to the architect who planned it, and under whose direction the whole work was accomplished. Therefore, the Corinthians are to consider Paul, or Apollos, or Cephas as nothing more than persons employed by the great Architect to form a building. This building is entirely designed by God. It will become a habitation of God through the Spirit. It is important to note that the Corinthians constitute God's building together. They are united in the same structure. There is no room for individualism in the body of Christ.

PAUL: THE SKILLED MASTER-BUILDER (3:10–17)

> 10 According to the grace of God which was given to me, like a wise master builder I laid a foundation, and another is building on it. But each man must be careful how he builds on it.
>
> 11 For no man can lay a foundation other than the one which is laid, which is Jesus Christ.
>
> 12 Now if any man builds on the foundation with gold, silver, precious stones, wood, hay, straw,

13 each man's work will become evident; for the day will show it because it is *to be* revealed with fire, and the fire itself will test the quality of each man's work.

14 If any man's work which he has built on it remains, he will receive a reward.

15 If any man's work is burned up, he will suffer loss; but he himself will be saved, yet so as through fire.

As a wise master-builder, an experienced man in architecture, Paul has laid the foundation by preaching Christ through the Grecian provinces. Those who come after him are to build according to the plan and grand design of the temple—a *design* or *plan* which is from God, making it imperative that all things must be done according to the *pattern* which he has exhibited. One thing that Paul seeks to make clear in the verse is that the building which is the church is not the work of any particular evangelist, preacher, or even an apostle. It is a group work. Although God has used Paul to lay the foundation, he acknowledges that others, such as Apollos, also build on this foundation of Christ. Then he gives a warning: Every builder—Paul, Apollos, and whoever works for God—must be careful how he builds. The shift in thought is now from the worker to his work. Here Paul refers to his own work (v. 11). The Corinthians had preferences for various leaders, but as Paul has previously said in 1:17 and 2:2, Jesus himself (rather than his followers) is the one irreplaceable foundation of the church. No church leader must be seen as having more than a strictly subordinate role. Leaders are to be respected, but not worshiped.

Unfortunately, there are situations where cultural norms seem to have trounced Biblical standards. This is especially true in many parts of Africa, where leaders have often exploited the exceptionally high respect that African people have for leadership. Moreover, although the workers cannot lay a foundation other than Christ, they had better be careful how they build on him. Any defects in their work will be their own fault. Christ cannot be blamed for it. Laying a foundation of a building does not translate to the ownership of the building, as many founders of "ministries" and "churches" seem to suggest. This brings to mind situations in many churches, particularly in Africa, where the founders/leaders of churches try to stifle dissent by making it very clear that they are the ones that the Lord gave the blueprints for their organizations/churches. As such, their decisions are not to be questioned.

1 Corinthians

It is clear in verse 12 that Paul wanted the preachers and teachers in the church to build a superstructure with the same material as the foundation. So, instead of talking about the details of the building itself, Paul turns his attention to the kind of materials Christian workers are using: preaching the cross for salvation, building up believers (cf. 1:18), and living a Christian life that reflects their preaching (2:2–4). So, Paul stresses that those contractors who employ inferior material will have the quality of their work exposed by the fire of God's judgment (v. 13). Paul means that it shall be clear what kind of materials every spiritual builder uses. God will test whether the doctrines preached produce genuine repentance, faith, and holiness in the hearers. There are numerous instances of the serious consequences that careless builders have had to face in the case of the collapse of buildings, particularly when it results in the loss of lives. In some instances, builders are taken to court and are subsequently required to pay heavy penalties and effect settlement to the plaintiffs. Similarly, God will hold leaders accountable for the type of preaching and teaching they engage in. Do their teachings build a solid, spiritual community? God will see whether the leaders provide a good model in how they live their lives and whether they offer good care and support to believers they are building into God's house. As fire purifies metals, and finds out and separates whatever dross is mixed with them; so shall the strict process of the final judgment test the work of every public teacher to see whether it came up to the Scripture standard. With Paul's eschatological framework that permeates his writings (cf. Rom 2:5, 16; 13:12; 1 Cor 1:8; 2 Cor 1:14; Phil 1:6; 1 Thess 5:2–9; 2 Thess 2:2), it is clear that the "day" refers to "the day of the Lord" (1 Thess 5:2), the day of the second coming of Christ (cf. 2 Thess 2:2). Paul's vision of final judgment agrees with those of the prophetic traditions of the Old Testament (Amos 5:18, 20; Mal 4:1).

In the modern church, there is an aversion to the preaching and hearing about God's jugdement. Such an attitude fails to grasp the truth that judgment and grace are inseparable parts of the gospel message. A popular televangelist in the United States recently said in an interview that he has nothing to do with the preaching of repentance and judgment. It is not surprising that 1 Corinthians 3:12–15, as well as other passages that speak of judgment, are left out by some when this passage is read in worship. But the message of the passage is clear. God will not tolerate divisiveness and pride. However, this particular passage is neither about "purgatory" or

THE CHURCH: THE TEMPLE OF GOD (3:16–17)

> 16 Do you not know that you are a temple of God and *that* the Spirit of God dwells in you?
>
> 17 If any man destroys the temple of God, God will destroy him, for the temple of God is holy, and that is what you are.

Paul has compared the Christian congregation at Corinth to a field (3:6–9) and then to a building (3:10–15). Now he compares them to a temple. It is important to note that when Paul says "you are the temple of God," he was speaking corporately, rather than individually. The whole Corinthian Church was the temple of God. Although made up of individuals, it is the church, corporately, that constitutes the body of Christ, a metaphor that Paul later expands on in chapter 12. The import of this verse is to show the danger that awaits someone who tears apart or destroys the church. God will not save such a person. The Corinthians must understand how special they were, and how their status as the temple of God demanded a particular kind of leadership and lifestyle. Furthermore, the imagery of the metaphor drives home the point that the divisive loyalties that plagued the church were not only contrary to the nature of leadership that is required in the church, but also were contrary to the nature of the church itself. The church is God's project. The imagery of the temple should force the church to think of how much of the presence of God is experienced when its members gather together, and to reflect seriously on what it means to be a holy community in an unholy world. A situation where members of the church bicker on such things as where to place a pulpit or a flowerpot, or where to sing contemporary songs or old hymns, belies the true nature of the church as one holy people.

FINAL WARNING ABOUT WISDOM (3:18–23)

> 18 Let no man deceive himself. If any man among you thinks that he is wise in this age, he must become foolish, so that he may become wise.

> 19 For the wisdom of this world is foolishness before God. For it is written, "*He is* the one who catches the wise in their craftiness";
>
> 20 and again, "The Lord knows the reasonings of the wise, that they are useless."
>
> 21 So then let no one boast in men. For all things belong to you,
>
> 22 whether Paul or Apollos or Cephas or the world or life or death or things present or things to come; all things belong to you,
>
> 23 and you belong to Christ; and Christ belongs to God.

Paul returns again to address the underlying problem of the church at Corinth—foolishness and wisdom. The Corinthians' immaturity prevented them from understanding the nature of God's work, it moved them away from the foundation of their faith. Quoting Job 5:13 and Psalm 94:11, Paul reinforces what he has previously said in chapters 1–3. In order to make the quotation more applicable to the Corinthians, Paul changed the word "human" to "wise." The Corinthians were then warned not to be proud of particular leaders. They are only human. The climax of Paul's discussion about the problem of division in the church ended with his exhortation to the Corinthians to focus on God. In our days, denominationalism is a great problem, as well as often a hindrance to the proclamation of the gospel.

The following question is always asked: who do you belong to? Paul made it clear to the Corinthians that they neither belonged to him nor to Apollos. It is not right for a church to replace the word of God with human wisdom and leaders. Men or women, committees, executives, and board members must never be allowed to take over the leadership of the Holy Spirit. God provides human leaders for his church. They are to build up the whole church in a spiritual way. However, when the churches or individual believers become enslaved, as it were, to human leadership (something I have seen to be prevalent in Africa, and particularly in my home country of Nigeria), they not only miss the blessing of God, but they mar the work of the churches, and this cannot be done with impunity.

QUESTIONS FOR PERSONAL REFLECTION

1. In light of Paul's rebuke of the Corinthians, should any believer delight in being a "carnal" or "merely human" Christian?

The Nature of Christian Leadership

2. What is the role of Christian leaders, and to what extent should believers exhibit their loyalties to their leaders?
3. How important is it to maintain the unity and purity of the church?
4. What do you consider as your personal role in promoting unity in the church?
5. Why should Christian workers avoid competition with each other, and how can they do so?
6. What are the characteristics in your personal life that mark you either as a mature or immature Christian? What do you think you could do to overcome the latter?

1 Corinthians 4:1–13

The Nature of Christian Leadership Part 2

THERE WAS A REAL problem between Paul and the Corinthians; they tended to look down on him and not respect his apostolic authority. In the previous chapters, particularly in the last three verses of chapter 3, Paul has been refuting an exaggerated estimate of himself and his fellow evangelists. Now he anticipates a couple of questions: "How then are we to think of you? What exactly is your role in the purpose of God?" The answers are provided in the text below. Paul is about to draw out some implications for the ways the Corinthians should respond to him as an apostle. As such, in carefully chosen words, Paul will show the Corinthians how to have proper regard, one that is neither too exalted nor not too low of himself and other Christian leaders. As it was in Paul's Corinth, it is popular today to denigrate leadership in different spheres of life, whether governmental, educational, or religious. Many ministers come to the end of their ministry with low self-esteem, and some leave the ministry to escape the stress. Christ's cause is hindered immeasurably by the continual criticism of God's servants. Thus, this chapter provides valuable insights into how a minister could cope with the problems associated with the lack of appreciation without having to quit.

LEADERS AND CRITICISM (4:1–5)

> 1 Let a man regard us in this manner, as servants of Christ and stewards of the mysteries of God.
> 2 In this case, moreover, it is required of stewards that one be found trustworthy.

> 3 But to me it is a very small thing that I may be examined by you, or by *any* human court; in fact, I do not even examine myself.
> 4 For I am conscious of nothing against myself, yet I am not by this acquitted; but the one who examines me is the Lord.
> 5 Therefore do not go on passing judgment before the time, *but wait* until the Lord comes who will both bring to light the things hidden in the darkness and disclose the motives of *men's* hearts; and then each man's praise will come to him from God.

Paul has explained what preachers are not, in order to show that people should not make themselves dependent on them., The apostle now declares what they are, so that church members do not judge them rashly. He does so first by speaking of himself and Apollos (us; cf. 6:6). Then he speaks singly of himself (me; 5:3). Ministers are to be regarded as Christ's subordinates and as stewards of the mysteries of God. The Greek word *hyperetes*, "stewards," literally means a person who acts as rower under the orders of someone. It evokes the image of a slave-in-charge. He/she is a person laboring freely in the service of others. Paul uses it to refer to the acting and laborious side of the Christian ministry. A master in the first-century AD may have had a trusted slave who directed the household and instructed other slaves in their tasks (Luke 12:42). So "steward" could be used for anyone entrusted with responsibility and therefore accountable to others. it implies that preachers are custodians and administrators of a truth that is not theirs, but their master's. The trust administered by them is the mysteries of God. This term, "mystery," denotes the plan of salvation in general (see on 2:7).

In verse 2, Paul turns to examine the character of those who are handling God's truth. They, including himself, must show themselves faithful. Paul wants to clarify the requirements of a servant and a steward. He says that it is required of them to be found trustworthy. It is a requirement, not an option. Those who are called must take time to reflect upon the great task that is ahead of them, as well as the integrity that is needed to characterize their lives as they fulfill those tasks. Servants and stewards must be trustworthy, because their task is greater than anything in this world. Trustworthiness is the benchmark for evaluation of leaders. The question is, "Are we worthy of the trust of God? Is He able to trust us with His message and His mysteries?" Personal accountability to God is required from every servant.

Paul moves on in verses 3 and 4 to express the truth that, since he is the Lord's servant and steward, it is to the Lord that he owes responsibility. It is the Lord who judges him for the quality of his service. Human judgment has little value. Even self-evaluation is unreliable, Paul says. Christ is the Lord of the conscience, and is the one who can evaluate it properly. Having said this, Paul shows the absurdity of the Corinthians' eagerness to evaluate his work and that of his fellow workers. If Paul exercises such restraint in evaluating his own work, how much more ought the Corinthians to abstain from such rash judgments? Paul implies that the Corinthians were already judging. Therefore, Paul tells them to wait until the proper time—that is, the time of the Lord's return. God has the right to judge, and he will do so. He will bring to light what darkness hides and disclose our inward motives. Those who have been faithful in the service of their Master will receive praise from him when he returns. Paul was confident. He does not think that the outcome of judgment will be negative. He has been faithful. When a minister can focus on the judgment seat of Christ, where he or she is confident of giving an account of his or her ministry before an all-knowing Lord, he or she can discount the tainted and biased criticisms of others.

LEADERS AS MODELS (4:6–13)

> 6 Now these things, brethren, I have figuratively applied to myself and Apollos for your sakes, so that in us you may learn not to exceed what is written, so that no one of you will become arrogant in behalf of one against the other.
>
> 7 For who regards you as superior? What do you have that you did not receive? And if you did receive it, why do you boast as if you had not received it?
>
> 8 You are already filled, you have already become rich, you have become kings without us; and indeed, *I* wish that you had become kings so that we also might reign with you.
>
> 9 For, I think, God has exhibited us apostles last of all, as men condemned to death; because we have become a spectacle to the world, both to angels and to men.
>
> 10 We are fools for Christ's sake, but you are prudent in Christ; we are weak, but you are strong; you are distinguished, but we are without honor.
>
> 11 To this present hour we are both hungry and thirsty, and are poorly clothed, and are roughly treated, and are homeless;
>
> 12 and we toil, working with our own hands; when we are reviled, we bless; when we are persecuted, we endure;

> 13 when we are slandered, we try to conciliate; we have become as the scum of the world, the dregs of all things, *even* until now.

Paul addresses the Corinthians with a language of endearment: brothers and sisters. He has previously shown to them, by using himself and Apollos as examples of ministers and their ministry (3:5–9), how to avoid rivalries. He now proceeds to tell them that they should do the same, that is, think of them properly, and not beyond what is written. Paul and Apollos had become occasions for pride among the Corinthians. Paul proffers his view on leadership so that the Corinthians may not go beyond what is written. He wants the Corinthians to live up to the guiding principle concerning leadership evaluation, as he did himself.

Paul proceeds to draw a sarcastic contrast between him and the pretensions of the Corinthians to be something, to have arrived, and the actual situation of the apostles whose disciples they are so proud to be. On the one hand, the Corinthians were proud and claimed to be spiritually rich. On the other hand, Paul and Apollos were weak, despised, and persecuted. Paul knows they had been given grace by God. The problem was that the Corinthians were boasting as if what they had was a result of their human accomplishments. He is surprised that they don't acknowledge God's gift. In God's kingdom, there are no self-made men or women. We are all there because of God's grace.

Paul provides another reason for rejecting pride by asking a series of rhetorical questions. The abrupt questions of verse 7 now lead to a sustained contrast between the way the Corinthians see themselves and Paul's own experience of what it means to be an apostle. Paul ridicules their conceit. As the Corinthians see themselves, they are already blessed with everything God has to give. They are spiritual millionaires, kings. They have arrived, even without any help from Paul. The Corinthians evidently thought they had reached full maturity, and were ruling rather than walking humbly with God. The word "already" is placed foremost and repeated. It expresses well the movement of this whole passage: "Now already!" Paul and the other apostles are still in a world of suffering, but at Corinth, the church already lives in full triumph. Their fullness consisted of self-satisfaction and contempt. The term "riches" alludes to the spiritual gifts which distinguished this church above all others., Paul had recognized them from the outset (1:5, 7). The rebuke applies, not to the fact of their possession of gifts, but to the feeling of pride which accompanied it. No one should be "puffed up" or look on others with contempt. Christians may indeed enjoy the gifts that are given to certain leaders and individuals, but they should never become attached to one leader to the point of disparaging another leader with lesser gifts.

Paul continues the irony that began in verse 8. Paul replies that in his opinion—he speaks mildly, using the expression "it seems to me"—God has not placed the apostles in as great a position as the Corinthians think they themselves are in. The irony is that the Corinthians were trying to "reign," while their spiritual fathers and examples were far from "reigning." The Corinthian Church felt it had reached the pinnacle of spiritual attainment. The church was self-satisfied; so it was not aware of any spiritual hunger. They even thought that they have surpassed their teachers.

In contrast to the Corinthians, Paul goes on to explain that God has publicly displayed the apostles as humble, despised men, worthy of death. Paul alludes to the gladiators who were presented as a spectacle in the games of the amphitheater, and whose blood and last agonies formed the joy of a whole population of spectators. He pictures himself and his fellow workers as condemned to death and led forth by a conqueror. By his use of "spectacle," he seems to be alluding to the figure of condemned men tortured and exposed to the wild animals in the Colosseum. They are also pictured as despised before the whole "world" (Greek *kosmos*) and the angelic hosts. Such suffering is not limited to Paul, but includes other prominent Christian workers who were associated with the apostles. Paul's point is that, unlike the Corinthians, the apostles, through their sufferings and the way they handled them, demonstrated or "showcased" the grace of God.

Paul's words in verse 10 come as the trenchant rebukes for the kind of religion Christianity was in danger of becoming in Corinth. The contrast between the two situations expressed in verses 8 and 9 is expressed in verse 10 in three antitheses, which are like blows for the arrogant Corinthians. These words are addressed especially to the leaders of the Corinthian congregation, but at the same time to all its members who share in the pretensions of these proud party leaders. Paul sets side by side once more the perception of the Christian life entertained by his readers and his own experience of apostolic ministry: *We are fools for the sake of Christ. We are weak, but you are strong. You are held in honor, but we in disrepute!* Words like "fools," "weak," and "disrepute" remind us of 1:25. There Paul showed that God's wisdom of the cross is foolishness in the eyes of the world. God's power, the power of the cross, is also weakness in the eyes of the world. So, although Paul may be a fool, he is a fool for Christ's sake. Though he may be weak, he is weak with Christ.

In verses 11–13, Paul goes on to describe in detail the hardships he and his fellow Christian workers have suffered throughout their ministry. Paul does not want to boast about his sufferings. He intends to highlight the misery of his outward circumstances in contrast to the self-sufficiency of the Corinthians. Paul's experience of apostolic ministry stands in the sharpest contrast to the Corinthians' perception of the Christian life. The story is told of the bishop of Singapore who was repeatedly beaten by his guards during the Second World War, whom he consciously forgave. Years later the bishop baptized and confirmed one of his torturers, having been greatly moved by the forgiveness shown to him. Paul and his fellow workers embody the wisdom of the cross. Had the Corinthians embodied that wisdom, they would begin to live peaceably among themselves, though they may be subject to the ridicule of outsiders.

CORRECTIONS: BASIS AND AIM (4:16–21)

> 14 I do not write these things to shame you, but to admonish you as my beloved children.
>
> 15 For if you were to have countless tutors in Christ, yet *you would* not *have* many fathers, for in Christ Jesus I became your father through the gospel.
>
> 16 Therefore I exhort you, be imitators of me.
>
> 17 For this reason I have sent to you Timothy, who is my beloved and faithful child in the Lord, and he will remind you of my ways which are in Christ, just as I teach everywhere in every church.
>
> 18 Now some have become arrogant, as though I were not coming to you.
>
> 19 But I will come to you soon, if the Lord wills, and I shall find out, not the words of those who are arrogant but their power.
>
> 20 For the kingdom of God does not consist in words but in power.
>
> 21 What do you desire? Shall I come to you with a rod, or with love and a spirit of gentleness?

The basis of Paul's appeal to the Corinthians is his relationship to them. They were his spiritual children. He was their father in the faith. So he had both the authority and experience to teach and rebuke them. Paul could boldly tell them to imitate him. His Christ-likeness and selfless service were evident to the Corinthians. Paul's desire was not for the Corinthians to be engaged in hero worship directed at him, but rather to emulate the spiritual qualities that they have observed in his life as their spiritual father. As a proof of his concern, Paul had sent Timothy to Corinth to assist and remind them of their relationship with Paul, as well as instruct them in God's truth. There were some in Corinth who thought that Paul was either shy or afraid to visit Corinth. But Paul's purpose was to come to them as God willed. He could come to them with either a rod for discipline or in love with meekness. The Corinthians must decide what they wanted.

QUESTIONS FOR PERSONAL REFLECTION

1. Based on this chapter, what are some of the qualifications of spiritual leaders?
2. How significant are the issues of faithfulness and accountability in ministry?
3. How would you measure your commitment to the gospel in the light of Paul's sufferings, and all that he willingly endured?
4. Is it good practice for Christians to evaluate their service for the Lord? If so, by what standards? What dangers are involved in self-evaluation, and how can they be avoided?
5. What should a member with a bad attitude toward the pastor do?

1 Corinthians 5:1–13

Discipline in the Church

Believers often speak in glowing terms about the early church's power and accomplishments, and rightly so. In fact, some people pray that they may have a church that looks like those in the New Testament. However, many fail to take into consideration that there were real problems in the first-century congregations. There were times when the early church suffered disappointments and encountered sin in its midst. Some of the problems in the Corinthian Church are addressed by Paul in the next three chapters. The Scriptures were written for our sake and spiritual help. It is important that they are carefully examined in order that present-day believers may avoid the failures of the early church while they strive to emulate its good points.

SIN IN THE CHURCH (5:1–2)

> 1 It is actually reported that there is immorality among you, and immorality of such a kind as does not exist even among the Gentiles, that someone has his father's wife.
>
> 2 You have become arrogant and have not mourned instead, so that the one who had done this deed would be removed from your midst.

One of the most deplorable conditions imaginable prevailed in the church at Corinth. To his dismay, Paul has heard reports of sexual immorality, immorality such as even pagans do not tolerate: the union of a man with his stepmother. One's "father's wife" is a designation in the Old Testament (see

Lev 18:8; 20:11). How shocking to realize the depths of unrighteousness to which this offender sank! His sin tarnished the testimony of the church.

What dismays Paul still further is the attitude taken to this irregularity by the Corinthians themselves. The attitude of the Corinthian believers toward the sin is appalling. They were not distressed in the least. Their sensitivity was not troubled. Far from going into mourning and turning the offender out of the community, as they should have done, they are actually proud of themselves, of their spiritual "attainments" and their superior wisdom and gifts, in spite of the presence of this serious immorality in their midst. The community appeared to take no responsibility for the conduct of its members. They refused to face the cancerous condition that worked its way through the vital organs of the church, daily destroying its testimony for Christ and its effectiveness with the gospel. Their gifts were unmatched, and so was their sin. What an irony!

JUDGMENT (DISCIPLINE) OF THE OFFENDER (5:3–5)

> 3 For I, on my part, though absent in body but present in spirit, have already judged him who has so committed this, as though I were present.
>
> 4 In the name of our Lord Jesus, when you are assembled, and I with you in spirit, with the power of our Lord Jesus,
>
> 5 *I have decided* to deliver such a one to Satan for the destruction of his flesh, so that his spirit may be saved in the day of the Lord Jesus.

Paul knows that orderly discipline is God's way of correcting saints and protecting the purity of the church. He would not allow the problem of sin to remain unresolved (5:3–5). He was zealous to uphold these purposes. His absence from Corinth did not prevent him condemning the immorality. Although absent, Paul has already reached his judgment on how the offender is to be dealt with. When they are all assembled in the name of our Lord Jesus, Paul himself being with them in spirit, through the power of our Lord Jesus, they are to pass judgment on the offender and carry out the sentence. Notice that the church was to take this disciplinary action, even though it was recommended and commanded by Paul. The community as a whole has to take action. The sentence which Paul enjoins is a severe one, but one which envisages ultimate deliverance. Discipline is not punishment.

CHRIST, OUR PASSOVER SACRIFICE (5:6–8)

> 6 Your boasting is not good. Do you not know that a little leaven leavens the whole lump *of dough*?
>
> 7 Clean out the old leaven so that you may be a new lump, just as you are *in fact* unleavened. For Christ our Passover also has been sacrificed.
>
> 8 Therefore let us celebrate the feast, not with old leaven, nor with the leaven of malice and wickedness, but with the unleavened bread of sincerity and truth.

Paul now moves to more general exhortation prompted by the reprehensible attitude which the Corinthians have taken in the case of the incestuous man. The Corinthian believers continued to be insensitive to the sin in their midst. They were too proud to recognize a blemish. Their pride was misplaced. Paul argues that any sin can permeate the ranks of the church and affect its entire life and usefulness. To drive home his point, he asks, "Do you not know that a little leaven leavens the whole lump?" The image of leaven was commonly used to describe something apparently insignificant, but capable of permeating and affecting a much larger entity of which it was part. As the Hebrews searched out leaven in the Passover season and purged their houses of all of it, so the believer and the churches must purge out sin. The Corinthians' acceptance of the scandalous situation in their midst is a sign of a moral blind spot which is capable of corrupting the life of the whole community.

Paul commands that the Corinthians *cleanse out* the old leaven of sin. This action is here regarded as a symbol of purging one's life of evil ways. The Corinthians are to get rid of the old leaven. The primary reference in the context is to the removal of the incestuous man, but the image is to be given a broader application in verse 8. They must remove the corrupting influence in their midst so that they would be a new lump of dough before it was touched by leaven. They were to bring their conduct up to their confession—"as you are really unleavened." Paul presents the feasts of Passover and Unleavened Bread as a type pointing to Christ and fulfilled in him. Thus, Paul can say that Christ has been sacrificed as our Passover lamb. Christ is the fulfillment of the old order. The moral cleansing signified by the annual cleansing of the household of old leaven is already eternally accomplished by Christ. Therefore, Paul can assure his readers that they already are unleavened dough.

Paul draws a conclusion from what he said in verse 7, depicting the Christian life as one which must be of celebration in Christ. It is a life of constant festival that demands constant purity. Believers must continuously keep "leaven" out of their lives and fellowship. Those things which characterized the unsaved state (old leaven) are to be put away. Malice (a vicious disposition) and evil speak of everything in believers that displease God. Sincerity and truth speak of purity, both in motives and deeds.

THE PREVIOUS LETTER (5:9–10)

> 9 I wrote you in my letter not to associate with immoral people;
> 10 I *did* not at all *mean* with the immoral people of this world, or with the covetous and swindlers, or with idolaters, for then you would have to go out of the world.

In his earlier letter, Paul had laid down that the Corinthians must have nothing to do with those who are sexually immoral. However, in maintaining church purity, Paul carefully sets out certain truths that believers should carefully note. Believers must watch their fellowship. They are not to associate with immoral people. The basic thought here is that there should be no friendly mixing between the Corinthians and those who violate the normal function of sex.

CAST OUT THE WICKED ONE (5:11–13)

> 11 But actually, I wrote to you not to associate with any so-called brother if he is an immoral person, or covetous, or an idolater, or a reviler, or a drunkard, or a swindler—not even to eat with such a one.
> 12 For what have I to do with judging outsiders? Do you not judge those who are within *the church*?
> 13 But those who are outside, God judges. Remove the wicked man from among yourselves.

Paul knows that the Corinthians could misinterpret his instruction to stop intimate fellowship with unbelievers. Our lives should show that grace has a sanctifying hold on our attitudes and actions. Christians must meet with

DISCIPLINE IN THE CHURCH

sinners. It would be impossible to avoid all contact with them. God does not expect Christians to avoid contact with this evil world. However, he does intend that we are to be kept pure while we are in the world. To avoid all contact with such people, the Christians of Corinth would have had to withdraw from society altogether. But that is not what Paul meant. He enlarges on what he has previously stated in verse 9, to include the covetous, those greedy of gain and quick to take advantage of others; the idolater; the railer; the drunkard; and the extortioner. Paul admonishes that Christians must have nothing to do with any so-called Christian who lived in such a fashion, and he refers to slanderers and drunkards, as further illustrations of the kind of misconduct he has in mind. They should not eat with anyone like that. To fellowship with the one living in sin would be to confirm his/her waywardness and become a party to it.

In verse 12, Paul clarifies the area of the church's disciplinary responsibility. It does not extend beyond the Christian community, and he himself disclaims any desire to pass any judgment on those outside it. God is their judge. The Christian's authority for judging does not extend to those outside the church but it includes those within. God has granted to believers in church responsibility of judgment toward those who are within the church. Those who are critical of proper church discipline are in reality robbing those who need it of the possibility of cleansed lives that can bring glory and honor to Christ. Failure by church authorities to exercise effective discipline in situations that demands such really amounts to a failure in love both towards the offender himself, his past and potential victims, and the body of Christ.

Echoing the language of Deuteronomy 17:7, Paul urges them to root out the wrongdoer from their community (v. 13). The responsible exercise of this discipline sometimes calls for the exclusion of an errant member from the fellowship, and it is precisely that sort of situation that the Corinthians are facing now. Paul's words in this chapter may sound harsh, coming as they do from the author of the hymn to love in chapter 13. What has become of the love which keeps no score of wrongs? Yet the contemporary church urgently needs a reminder that discipline is an essential ingredient of love. Perhaps the reason that the modern church does not exercise discipline is due in part to its failure to see sin as a great threat to its spiritual health, or in part because people consider excommunication as too harsh and an unloving act. No wonder then that when, in recent years, prominent priests and ministers have been found guilty of sexual misconduct and financial impropriety, the reaction of church authorities has all too often been to cover the matter up, counsel the priests or ministers concerned to be more careful in the future, and transfer them elsewhere. At other times, the offender may be treated as a sick person in need of some form of therapy rather than as a sinner who needs to repent. Certainly anyone who advocates firmer action, closer to that advocated by Paul in this passage, is likely to be accused of vindictiveness and witch-hunting. Paul's point in this chapter is to show how important the church is and, particularly, how its purity should be guarded. God values the church to the extent that he commands us to put out those who endanger its purity. Therefore, we ought to love, respect, and develop a greater appreciation for the safety it provides us from Satan.

QUESTIONS FOR PERSONAL REFLECTION

1. How would you feel if your pastor, best friend, or the person who led you to Christ were to be caught carrying on sexual immorality with one of his or her parents? Shocked, disgusted or grieved, or open-minded?

2. What should be the ultimate goal of discipline? Does your church have a process of restoration of erring believers?

3. How can we win immoral persons to Christ without violating our own separation from sin and worldly practices?

4. What is the role of the community in safeguarding the purity of the church?

5. What factors rob the church of its power today?

1 Corinthians 6:1–20

Christians in Pagan Courts

"THE NEW TESTAMENT TEACHING standards are wonderful, but where are those who live up to them? Are there any folk in the world who do? Are there any living the Christian life? Can this book really produce that which it sets forth?" These words and the questions were reportedly uttered and asked by David Ben-Gurion, a former prime minister of Israel to a missionary. These were questions that were pertinent, given the lifestyle of the Corinthians and their profession of their faith in Christ. There was a clear credibility gap between who the Corinthians professed they were and how they lived. Their behaviors did not reflect their belief. There was a disconnect between their confession and their conduct. They lived in such a manner that must have left the unbelievers among them wondering whether they were any different. It is probably right to suggest that similar questions, as Ben-Gurion asked, continue to echo in the minds of many people of the world today. In the same way as the Corinthians, carnality continues to reveal itself in various forms. Division is rampant in the church. As a matter of irony, churches continue to multiply by division. Also, church members continue to be indifferent to immorality and would rather turn a blind eye than deal with it. As we see in 1 Corinthians 6, it troubled Paul for obvious reasons. It was so abhorrent to the spirit of Christianity for believers to haul their brethren before heathen magistrates for the adjudication of their differences. It is difficult for two believers to engage in a legal suit with one another without bringing damage to the church before the community. This practice has become too common, even today. Property disputes, damage suits, unpaid bills, or worse yet, divided churches—all of these tend to lessen the world's respect for Christians and their churches. The goal of believers must not be to "get their due," or to "get even," but to honor their Savior and to bring men and women to him. In 1 Corinthians 6:1-11, Paul addresses the issue of lawsuits before pagan judges. Paul is especially aggravated by the fact that, firstly, they have so little understanding of who they are in Christ (1 Cor 6:2-4), and secondly, that this way of acting so thoroughly destroys the witness of Corinthian community before the world (1 Cor 6:6). The failure of the people involved is primarily a failure of the church to live up to her calling as the people of God. Crucial to the whole argument is Paul's view of the Christian community as God's eschatological people, a view which Paul argues must determine its lifestyle in the present age.

CONFLICTS AMONG THE SAINTS (6:1-8)

> 1 Does any one of you, when he has a case against his neighbor, dare to go to law before the unrighteous and not before the saints?
>
> 2 Or do you not know that the saints will judge the world? If the world is judged by you, are you not competent *to constitute* the smallest law courts?
>
> 3 Do you not know that we will judge angels? How much more matters of this life?
>
> 4 So if you have law courts dealing with matters of this life, do you appoint them as judges who are of no account in the church?
>
> 5 I say *this* to your shame. *Is it* so, *that* there is not among you one wise man who will be able to decide between his brethren,
>
> 6 but brother goes to law with brother, and that before unbelievers?
>
> 7 Actually, then, it is already a defeat for you, that you have lawsuits with one another. Why not rather be wronged? Why not rather be defrauded?
>
> 8 On the contrary, you yourselves wrong and defraud. *You do* this even to *your* brethren.

It is neither unusual nor necessarily sinful to have differences of opinion. What matters is the attitude that may be developed and, consequently, expressed due to the differences. This is the issue at stake in this chapter. Paul expresses dismay at the thought that a believer who had a grievance against another should go to law, instead of having the matter resolved within the Christian community. Paul's shock is expressed in his statement "Does he dare?"—that is, "How dare he?" or "How in the world could that be?" For

Paul, such an attitude is an admission of Christian failure as well as a lack of understanding of the nature of the Body of Christ. Paul's sharp rebuke shows that the action was incompatible with Christianity. Although not overtly stated here, at issue among these believers is the problem of love and forgiveness. The settling of inter-Christian differences by going to court was contrary to the best interests of the individual family and church. There are times when questions of law are involved when it is necessary to determine the legal action to be taken. Paul did not forbid such. What he was saying was that it was wrong for two Christians to become so involved in acute misunderstanding that they want to go to a heathen court to decide who was right. The story is told of a pastor who unintentionally made a statement that angered one of his deacons. The deacon led him to the door, pushed him out of the house, and slammed the door in his face. As the pastor walked to his car, he became very angry and resentful. However, he had a change of attitude, humbled himself, returned immediately to the deacon's door, and asked for forgiveness. The result was unity and forgiveness instead of bitterness and division.

Paul now addresses the entire community, referring to common knowledge: "Do you not know?" Paul says that since believers will judge the world, they must not feel incompetent to judge themselves. It is part of their vocation. It is important to note that by addressing the whole congregation, Paul shows the implication of one person's sin for the entire community. Sin is never simply a private or personal matter. The action of the "one" affects the "all"—that is, the community should not have allowed the incident.

To underscore what he just said in verse 2, Paul goes further to say that not only would believers judge the world, but also they would judge the angels (6:3–6). He says, "Do you not know that we are to judge angels?" The question heightens the absurdity of the Corinthians' behavior. If believers are to judge angels, then they should be able to handle the "trivial" matters and disputes that confront them on a daily basis. The Corinthians brought their cases before "outsiders with no standing in the church," a language that Paul uses to accentuate the difference between those who are believers and those who are not. Paul's point is simply that Christians not only own a different allegiance, but also are called to live by radically different standards from those of the world. The Corinthian Christians had remained babes too long. It was time for them for them to display some spiritual maturity. Summing it up, Paul rebukes them in sharp words: "I say this to your shame." There is enough harm wrought in the Christian household when two believers wrangle with one another, but it is considerably worse when they wrangle publicly before the unsaved. What an irony that the Corinthian Church which boasted of its wisdom had no one among them that was wise enough to decide matters between their members.

In verse 7, Paul points out that the situation of the Corinthians was that of spiritual deficiency (carnality). He questioned them, asking why (since settlement was so difficult and perhaps sometimes impossible) they did not relinquish their rights, and even allow themselves to be defrauded, rather than rush into heathen courts. Spiritual Christianity is conciliatory, and those who strive and work for reconciliation magnify Jesus Christ. If the very community which claims to be the object and instrument of the reconciliation of God is itself unreconciled, its credibility is called into question. Although Paul now addresses more directly the initiator of the legal action, his use of the plural form of the verb shows that he is still concerned about the community as a whole in asking whether it would not be much better to submit and let oneself be defrauded than to take such action. One can detect here, as elsewhere (cf. Rom 12:14, 17, 21), an awareness on Paul's part of the teaching of Jesus on repaying evil with good.

Paul now directs his focuses at the member who perpetrated the original wrong (v. 8). Long experience has shown that some of the condemnable practices in the Corinthian Church have survived to this time. On the one hand, there have been Christian tenants who have failed to pay rents to Christian owners and abused the premises while living there. In some instances, money has been borrowed from trusting Christians with a promise to repay in "six months." Not only was the borrowed money not repaid in the required time, but the borrower also justified his/her failure to repay the debt due to hard times, thus injuring or defrauding a Christian brother/sister. On the other hand, there are well-to-do Christians who have taken undue advantage of less privileged ones under the guise of helping them. Such acts are deplorable. Paul's use of the plural indicates that his outrage is directed equally at the community, which has allowed this scandalous train of events to run its course.

THE KINGDOM OF GOD AND
THE "UNRIGHTEOUS" (6:9–11)

> 9 Or do you not know that the unrighteous will not inherit the kingdom of God? Do not be deceived; neither fornicators, nor idolaters, nor adulterers, nor effeminate, nor homosexuals,
>
> 10 nor thieves, nor *the* covetous, nor drunkards, nor revilers, nor swindlers, will inherit the kingdom of God.
>
> 11 Such were some of you; but you were washed, but you were sanctified, but you were justified in the name of the Lord Jesus Christ and in the Spirit of our God.

Paul backs his rebuke up with a warning. The Corinthian Christians conduct was so deplorable that Paul considered it necessary and wise to remind them that unrighteous persons do not inherit God's kingdom. He goes on to list some of the sins from which the Corinthians have been cleansed. Paul's point is that the transforming experience that the Corinthians have experienced is belied by the problem of litigation that was going on. They are now a "new creation" (cf. 2 Cor 5:17). Paul's demand for a different style of life among the Corinthian congregation is to be predicated on the church's awareness of its own character as a washed, sanctified, and justified people.

A transformed moral life ought to be a result of a transforming experience. Here Paul uses three different images for the same experiential reality: conversion to Christ. The believer has entered upon a new state of existence as he now relates to the Lord Jesus Christ (cf. 1 Cor 1:2) and the Spirit of God. The believer has participated in that separation from sin and obedient commitment to God, which was characteristic of Christ Jesus. It involves a relational change. It is to be separated from a former life to experience a new life. When Paul here affirms that the Corinthians have been sanctified, it is in the context of complete changes that have occurred in their lives from an ethical standpoint. Because they have been sanctified, they have changed from a life of idolatry to the worship of Christ, from immorality to a life governed by the principles of Christ and his Spirit. For someone to claim to have experienced grace and yet engage in the kind of practices earlier described in the chapter is, to Paul, an absurdity. For Paul, grace and obedience are like inseparable sides of a coin; or conjoined twins, one of which cannot survive without the other. Nothing is so effective in reaching others as a transformed life.

A believer (formerly a heavy smoker and drunkard) was telling his neighbors at their annual community party what the Lord had done for him in saving him from the power of sin. He spoke with humility, hoping to win some of his former drinking partners for Christ. One scoffed, telling him that he (the new believer) was dreaming, and he would wake up and be back with them in a few days. The believer's son quietly whispered to his dad, "I sure hope he doesn't wake up then, because our family likes what the Lord has done for our dad." There is transforming power in the gospel. It transformed the Corinthians. It still transforms today.

PURITY, FREEDOM, AND THE BODY (6:12–20)

> 12 All things are lawful for me, but not all things are profitable. All things are lawful for me, but I will not be mastered by anything.
>
> 13 Food is for the stomach and the stomach is for food, but God will do away with both of them. Yet the body is not for immorality, but for the Lord, and the Lord is for the body.
>
> 14 Now God has not only raised the Lord, but will also raise us up through His power.
>
> 15 Do you not know that your bodies are members of Christ? Shall I then take away the members of Christ and make them members of a prostitute? May it never be!
>
> 16 Or do you not know that the one who joins himself to a prostitute is one body *with her*? For He says, "The two shall become one flesh."
>
> 17 But the one who joins himself to the Lord is one spirit *with Him*.
>
> 18 Flee immorality. Every *other* sin that a man commits is outside the body, but the immoral man sins against his own body.
>
> 19 Or do you not know that your body is a temple of the Holy Spirit who is in you, whom you have from God, and that you are not your own?
>
> 20 For you have been bought with a price: therefore glorify God in your body.

What is freedom, and how does it relate to sexual purity and the believer's use of his or her body? These are the issues Paul is about to address in this section. First Corinthians 6:12–20 addresses a case of fornication (a broad term used for all forms of sexual impurity) in the Corinthian Church. The Corinthians have failed to exercise sexual purity (6:13–20), once again thinking that their freedom in Christ meant license to sin (6:12). But since they had been bought at great cost, and their bodies were the temple of the Holy Spirit, they ought not to go beyond the bounds of true grace.

Paul sets the stage for his argument in the section by twice quoting a Corinthian slogan, "all things are lawful," a phrase that suggests the carefree attitude of the Corinthians. But he quickly adds, "but not all things are beneficial," and "but I will not be dominated by anything." Thus, Paul insists that freedom is shown in doing what is beneficial to others (v. 12a), what demonstrates the resurrection power in the life of the individual (v. 14), what expresses being part of Christ's body (v. 15), and what shows the believer's new identity as a "temple of the Holy Spirit." Moreover, Paul reinterprets the freedom of the individual by setting it firmly in the wider context of significance and obligation. The union of the believer with a prostitute is wrong and disorderly because it violates and contradicts the most important union of all: that between the Lord and the Lord's people. Paul endeavors to put right not only the understanding of freedom held by the Corinthians, but also their attitude to the body. Among many Christian circles today, any slight mention of the believer's responsibility to take care of the physical body, or to avoid certain practices, is immediately labeled as legalism. It is clear from the Scriptures that one does not fulfill certain requirements apart from repentance and faith in Christ in order to obtain salvation. Nevertheless, it is also wrong to have the carefree attitude of "it doesn't matter," whatever one does, after salvation. A believer should always ask questions such as "How does my action affect my brother or sister?" or "Is my action edifying?"—that is, "Does it build up the body of Christ?" For Paul, freedom was neither absolute nor freedom from unclear. Instead, freedom is found in our relationship with the Lord and his saints. This understanding of freedom becomes clearer in Paul's discussion of idol food in chapters 8-10. Yet, it must be said that Christian freedom goes beyond the concern for others. It must be exercised responsibly and not lead to enslavement.

In verse 13, Paul affirms that the body is not meant for immorality. It is important that as he moves from the question of food to that of sexuality, Paul introduces the term "body" in order for the Corinthians to know that the physical body and its activities such as sex are not immaterial to the life of freedom in the kingdom of God. The body is more than physical organs—it is a whole person capable of relationship. As such, bodily existence, as Paul understands it, connotes existence for others; e.g., being in relationship. The body has a purpose. It is for the Lord—that is, it is the instrument in which we serve God. Because of the body's relation to the Lord, it must not be given to immorality. Moreover, the body is destined for resurrection. As such, Paul could say, "And God raised the Lord and will also raise us up by his power."

The nature of the relationship between the believer's body and Christ, and the consequential incompatibility between that relationship and union with a prostitute, is further detailed. Our bodies are members of Christ! What a staggering statement with great ethical implications. That which belongs to Christ cannot be surrendered for fornication. Paul hints at the concept of the church as the body of Christ, which is to be developed in 10:16–17; 11:27–34; and 12:12–31. Paul heightens the argument by referring to Genesis 2:24. To join with a harlot is to become one with him or her. It is totally unacceptable. Hence Paul commands the Corinthians to "shun immorality." The word translated "shun" (NRSV) ia better translated as "keep on fleeing."

Verses 20 and 21 are the climax of Paul's argument in this section. Believers constitute the temple of God both personally and corporately. Paul has earlier used the same imagery in 1 Corinthians 3:16 (see discussion in that place). Therefore, for the presence of God to remain with them, there is a need for purity. Believers are to glorify God in their bodies. This is a timely reminder to Christians in the twenty-first century that our bodies are to be holy and engaged in the pursuits of only such things as glorify God. The body belongs to God both by right of creation and redemption. So the Christian must glorify God in all the uses of the body. Fornication, prostitution, drunkenness, and uncleanness must not exist among God's children. Today believers are surrounded with unsolicited pornographic advertisements on the television and billboards, sexually explicit plays and movies on television, trash talk on the radio, materialism, and idolatry in the guise of cultural revival, etc. We too live in a day of moral depression as the Corinthians. The Corinthians were to flee the things that confronted them. So must we. They were also to stand with lives of purity in a pagan community for Jesus Christ in such a way as to bring praise to him (cf. 1 Pet 2:10–11). So do we. The question is, shall we follow the world, or follow the Lord? We need to ensure that we do not adjust our lives to the shifting standards of the world. Instead, we must remain true to God at all costs and adorn the gospel of our Savior and Lord, Jesus Christ.

QUESTIONS FOR PERSONAL REFLECTION

1. Why does Paul consider it shameful for believers to be involved in litigations?

2. What is the importance of Paul's discussion for conflict resolution in the church in this chapter?

3. Is everything permissible for believers? What are the implications of Paul's statement that "all things are lawful but not all things are beneficial" for Christian living, particularly among people of other faiths?

4. What does it mean to be dominated? Was Paul referring to only things that dominated the body, or also to things which dominate us in other ways? Is there anything in your life that dominates you?

5. How do you define sexual immorality? Why would Paul advocate fleeing sexual immorality instead of simply resisting it? How easy has it been for you to resist sexual immorality?

1 Corinthians 7:1–40

Marriage and Sexual Relations

UP TO THIS POINT, Paul has been dealing with issues he had heard about from others, but now he begins answering some specific questions they sent him in the form of a letter. The discussion in this chapter is neither a comprehensive teaching of Paul on marriage nor a systematic guide to marriage and the family. There are, nevertheless, some instructions and guidelines that could help believers today. Which type of lifestyle is best for being a follower of Jesus Christ? Is it better to be married or to be single? Is it better to stay married to an unbeliever or divorce them? How about sex and spirituality? These are the types of questions Paul addresses in the chapter.

QUESTION ONE: SEX AND SPIRITUALITY (7:1–6)

1 Now concerning the things about which you wrote, it is good for a man not to touch a woman.

2 But because of immoralities, each man is to have his own wife, and each woman is to have her own husband.

3 The husband must fulfill his duty to his wife, and likewise also the wife to her husband.

4 The wife does not have authority over her own body, but the husband *does*; and likewise also the husband does not have authority over his own body, but the wife *does*.

5 Stop depriving one another, except by agreement for a time, so that you may devote yourselves to prayer, and come together again so that Satan will not tempt you because of your lack of self-control.

MARRIAGE AND SEXUAL RELATIONS

> 6 But this I say by way of concession, not of command.

There were some in Corinth who, because of the rampant sexual immorality of the day, equated sexual behavior with sin. And so they asked Paul if being a Christian meant they needed to live a celibate lifestyle, even if they were married. Paul gives them a clear answer. It is not "more spiritual" to live as married people, but to abstain from sexual relations. In fact, it will most likely lead to sinful behavior. Rather than agreeing that they should stop sexual relations, Paul presents quite a radical sexual ethic for the day: equality in the bedroom! Yet Paul could not be termed as a radical feminist. Paul exhorts husbands and wives to willingly give themselves to their spouses. God designed sex, and he meant for married people to enjoy it as a tool for increased intimacy between them. His advice to married people was this: Enjoy the sexual benefits of marriage, and serve God where you are.

QUESTION TWO: WHAT ABOUT CELIBACY? (7:7–9)

> 7 Yet I wish that all men were even as I myself am. However, each man has his own gift from God, one in this manner, and another in that.
>
> 8 But I say to the unmarried and to widows that it is good for them if they remain even as I.
>
> 9 But if they do not have self-control, let them marry; for it is better to marry than to burn *with passion*.

Was Paul a "woman hater," or was he an ascetic, or something of the monastic type? The simple answer to all these questions is no. As Paul looked at the matter of celibacy, he simply said that it was good. It has its advantages and is profitable. He agreed that it was good, but not for all people, and not at all times. He gave no commands and made no comparison, such as "marriage is good but celibacy is better." Just as it is not "more spiritual" for a married couple to deprive themselves of the sexual relationship with each other, so it is not "more spiritual" for a single person to remain single just for the point of trying to be a good Christian. Throughout history, there have been people known as "ascetics" who believe that the way to spiritual maturity is through the denial of anything the physical body finds pleasurable. They advocate only eating certain bland foods, only dressing in bland clothing with bland colors, and they believe that denying sexual urges elevates one to a higher spiritual plane. Paul mentions that certain individuals are given the gift of singleness and are able to control their sexual desires. For these people, Paul says it is better for them to stay unmarried (just as he himself is).

QUESTION THREE: WHAT ABOUT DIVORCE? (7:10–11)

> 10 But to the married I give instructions, not I, but the Lord, that the wife should not leave her husband
> 11 (but if she does leave, she must remain unmarried, or else be reconciled to her husband), and that the husband should not divorce his wife.

Some married Corinthians probably felt that they will be able to serve the Lord better if they are not married, so they probably thought of divorce. Paul reminds them that it is not God's will for Christians to separate from each other in order to be freed to serve him more effectively. In our time, some may think that they are called to serve as missionaries in a foreign country or have a particular ministry, but their spouses disagree. Questions such as "Shouldn't I pursue this calling for the sake of the kingdom, even though it means divorcing my spouse?" may come to mind at such a time. Paul's answer is a categorical, emphatic no. It is never God's will that one divorce a spouse in order to free oneself to serve him. What Christians ought to do is serve the Lord in the situation where they find themselves, though it may be less than ideal or desired.

QUESTION FOUR: SHOULD OLD RELATIONSHIPS CONTINUE AFTER CONVERSION? (7:12–16)

> 12 But to the rest I say, not the Lord, that if any brother has a wife who is an unbeliever, and she consents to live with him, he must not divorce her.
> 13 And a woman who has an unbelieving husband, and he consents to live with her, she must not send her husband away.
> 14 For the unbelieving husband is sanctified through his wife, and the unbelieving wife is sanctified through her believing husband; for otherwise your children are unclean, but now they are holy.
> 15 Yet if the unbelieving one leaves, let him leave; the brother or the sister is not under bondage in such *cases*, but God has called us to peace.

> 16 For how do you know, O wife, whether you will save your husband? Or how do you know, O husband, whether you will save your wife?

Paul now turns to those who were married before their conversion and who probably thought that their newfound faith and status in Christ demanded or required them to divorce their unbelieving spouses. They probably felt that living with an unbelieving spouse was detrimental to their Christian development or was limiting them in their service. Paul's answer is to stay together if the non-Christian is willing. Believers have been given an important role of bringing holiness to their marriages and families. As the only Christians in the family, believers have the privilege and obligation to show the love, acceptance, and forgiveness of Christ to their spouses, and may even get the opportunity to lead them to receiving Christ as their Savior! Therefore the believer is not to leave the non-Christian spouse in order to be a better Christian. As Paul would say, "Serve the Lord where you are!" One must realize that Paul was addressing monogamous situations. There is no record that polygamy was a prevalent practice in the Greco-Roman society in which Paul lived and ministered, particularly in Corinth. But Paul further advises those who are married to unbelievers. He says that if the non-Christian leaves, they should be allowed to go. Yet, as much as possible, "God wants his children to live in peace" (v. 15) with an unbelieving spouse. The thrust of Paul's argument in this section is clear: Conversion to Christianity is not to be used as a pretext for divorce or as an excuse to upset a marital harmony that previously existed.

A GENERAL PRINCIPLE: REMAIN AS YOU ARE (7:17–24)

> 17 Only, as the Lord has assigned to each one, as God has called each, in this manner let him walk. And so I direct in all the churches.
>
> 18 Was any man called *when he was already* circumcised? He is not to become uncircumcised. Has anyone been called in uncircumcision? He is not to be circumcised.
>
> 19 Circumcision is nothing, and uncircumcision is nothing, but *what matters is* the keeping of the commandments of God.
>
> 20 Each man must remain in that condition in which he was called.

> 21 Were you called while a slave? Do not worry about it; but if you are able also to become free, rather do that.
>
> 22 For he who was called in the Lord while a slave, is the Lord's freedman; likewise he who was called while free, is Christ's slave.
>
> 23 You were bought with a price; do not become slaves of men.
>
> 24 Brethren, each one is to remain with God in that *condition* in which he was called.

This section provides the theological basis for Paul's argument in the entire chapter, which is to "remain as you are." Some Corinthians thought that by divorce they may become spiritual. Instead, Paul argues that the call of God transcends all relationships and one's situation in life. For Paul, it makes no difference whether or not a person is single or married, poor or rich. One must live the Christian life as it should, regardless of whatever situation one is called into. This is what Paul states in verse 17 and reinstates in verses 22 and 23. The general call referred to by Paul is their salvation. Hence, Paul declares that circumcision or lack of it is not what commends one to God (Rom 2:25–29; Gal 5:6; 6:15). The important thing is to keep God's commands right where you are, in the situation you find yourself. We sometimes think that the grass would be greener if we were in some different situation, or we would be able to serve God more effectively if our life situation changed somehow. Although Paul makes a qualified exception in verse 21, it still is clear that being either slave or free is inconsequential in terms of one's relationship with the Lord.

QUESTION FIVE: VIRGINS, MARRIAGE, SEX, AND WIDOWS (7:25–40)

> 25 Now concerning virgins I have no command of the Lord, but I give an opinion as one who by the mercy of the Lord is trustworthy.
>
> 26 I think then that this is good in view of the present distress, that it is good for a man to remain as he is.
>
> 27 Are you bound to a wife? Do not seek to be released. Are you released from a wife? Do not seek a wife.
>
> 28 But if you marry, you have not sinned; and if a virgin marries, she has not sinned. Yet such will have trouble in this life, and I am trying to spare you.

Marriage and Sexual Relations

29 But this I say, brethren, the time has been shortened, so that from now on those who have wives should be as though they had none;

30 and those who weep, as though they did not weep; and those who rejoice, as though they did not rejoice; and those who buy, as though they did not possess;

31 and those who use the world, as though they did not make full use of it; for the form of this world is passing away.

32 But I want you to be free from concern. One who is unmarried is concerned about the things of the Lord, how he may please the Lord;

33 but one who is married is concerned about the things of the world, how he may please his wife,

34 and *his interests* are divided. The woman who is unmarried, and the virgin, is concerned about the things of the Lord, that she may be holy both in body and spirit; but one who is married is concerned about the things of the world, how she may please her husband.

35 This I say for your own benefit; not to put a restraint upon you, but to promote what is appropriate and *to secure* undistracted devotion to the Lord.

36 But if any man thinks that he is acting unbecomingly toward his virgin *daughter*, if she is past her youth, and if it must be so, let him do what he wishes, he does not sin; let her marry.

37 But he who stands firm in his heart, being under no constraint, but has authority over his own will, and has decided this in his own heart, to keep his own virgin *daughter*, he will do well.

38 So then both he who gives his own virgin *daughter* in marriage does well, and he who does not give her in marriage will do better.

39 A wife is bound as long as her husband lives; but if her husband is dead, she is free to be married to whom she wishes, only in the Lord.

40 But in my opinion she is happier if she remains as she is; and I think that I also have the Spirit of God.

Paul returns to answer the questions of the Corinthians about sex and marriage. In this section, he focuses on virgins, the married, and widows. Although he claiming not to have a direct word from the Lord on the subject he is about to address, he believes his thinking is faithful because of the Lord's mercy. And, as he says in verse 40, his thinking is guided by the Spirit. Specifically, Paul addresses the virgins (Greek *parthenos*, specifically refers to virgin women), suggesting that because of the "present necessity"

1 CORINTHIANS

(a better translation than "impending crisis" in NRSV), they should remain as they are. Scholars are not agreed on what Paul means by "present necessity." There are two main interpretations:

1. Some eschatological sufferings that Paul expects to come upon the church. This is what informs the translation of the word *enestosan* as "impending" rather than "present." The use of the same word as "present" in 3:22 suggests that the latter is better. The greater difficulty is with the word *anagke* translated as "crisis." The ordinary meaning of the word is "necessity" or "urgency." This is the same word that Paul uses in 9:16 and translated as "necessity" in the KJV.

2. An urgent imperative of proclaiming the gospel. In light of our discussion, it seems better to understand the present necessity that Paul refers to as the proclamation of the gospel. This interpretation better coheres with verse 26 and verses 32–35. Because of the shortness of time, the believer's energy should be devoted to the proclamation of the gospel.

But Paul isn't just talking to singles in this passage. He goes further, speaking in general terms to the married and the unmarried. All should live free from anxious care and concentrate on the things of the Lord. He calls all believers, regardless of marital status, to live with a sense of urgency because the time is short (v. 29).

It is a fact of life that we all get easily distracted. Think about how many times you have walked into a room and asked yourself what you are doing there! You knew that you came to the room for a reason, but you forgot what it was because you became distracted by something else. It is hard to remain focused. It is perhaps even harder to remain passionate about something. As believers in Christ, we want to stay focused on Jesus Christ—living for him, sharing his love with others, leading others to him, worshiping him. But we are often distracted or anxious about responsibilities, tasks, people, or entertainment that threatens to suck all the passion from our commitment to living for Jesus Christ and sharing him others before he returns. We need to recapture such a sense of urgency, apparent in Paul's words. One must ask if these verses prescribe celibacy or exalt it as a higher state of spirituality. Again, the answer is no. However, it is clear that Paul sees it as preferable to marriage in that it has the potential of freeing the time, attention, and energy of believers for the urgent all-important task of evangelization that must be done in the precious short interval before the second coming of Christ. For Paul, although the celibate life is not mandatory, it is nevertheless a life that has dignity and value before God. Paul is a well-balanced preacher-theologian. Paul will probably say to us today, "Remain and serve God in your calling!"

The last two verses both answer the question of remarriage by widows and divorcees and constitute a conclusion to the chapter. In closing, Paul once again expresses his preference for the single state by urging the Corinthians to remain as they were. He specifically addresses the Corinthian women who probably wanted to divorce their husbands, as well as widows who were contemplating marriage. Paul's opinion is that the widow will be more blessed, or better off (literally, "happier") as she is. Once again, one must note that, in referring to his own judgment or opinion, as he did in verse 25, Paul seems to reiterate that he was not about to impose his own view. However, Paul was also confident that his judgment was informed or guided by the Spirit.

QUESTIONS FOR PERSONAL REFLECTION

1. Do you think Christian ministers would be better and more successful shepherds if they were unmarried?
2. Is it more spiritual to be celibate? Does Paul command celibacy?
3. How should the problem of remarriage be solved in light of 1 Corinthians 7:8–9?
4. Given that the time is short according to Paul, how should believers live?
5. What should guide the Christian's cohabitation with an unbelieving spouse after conversion?

1 Corinthians 8:1–13

Christian Liberty and the Common Good

DO YOU THINK YOU have problems in the Lord's ministry? Think of those that Paul faced with the Corinthian believers. And he was supposed to provide the answers to all of their questions. Some believers think that the pastor or the leader has all the answers to every problem! Sometimes one can point to a definite answer from the Scriptures and say, "This is what God says about the problem." However, on other occasions, we have to apply a principle found in Scripture to a specific question in order to settle the matter. Decisions are a normal part of living. Every day, we are confronted with what to do in any number of ways, Some decisions are inconsequential, and some are important. Will your action and decision detract from your Christian testimony? Will what you do be unworthy of the name of Christ? What will be the impact of my action or behavior on others? Will it serve as an encouragement, or will it be a stumbling block to others?

History records that Greeks and Romans had integrated the worship of their pagan gods into the entire fabric of their national and domestic life. Small altars were erected in homes, and statutes were placed in gardens. The temple ceremonies, state occasions, festival events, and even family gatherings involved the sacrifices of animals to the pagan gods (idols) of the day. These things posed serious problems for the Christians in Corinth. At a family reunion, for example, an offering would be made to the gods, and part of the offering would be prepared for the reunion. What should Christians do? Should Christians eat meats that were sacrificed to idols, and risk offending God and other Christians? Or should they refuse and risk offending their family? If a believer was invited to a state function, would they eat of the meat first sanctified and then offered on such occasions? Would Christians risk offending the state official, or perhaps even the representative of Caesar? If Christians did partake of such food without scruple, with no struggle with their conscience, what about their fellow believers? Would they judge these actions as sinful? Would the Christian with a weaker conscience act on the basis of what he saw his brother or sister in Christ do, and yet suffer in conscience for it and experience a sense of disobedience little known to the one who can act out of Christian liberty with no remorse? Virtually all of the meat available for purchase came from animals which had been offered on the altar of a pagan god. Moreover, probably most of the gentile Christians of Corinth had been attending such banquets all their lives prior to their conversion. This is in contrast to the Corinthian Jewish Christians, who must have argued against meats as unclean. Therefore, the Corinthians asked Paul for his counsel regarding these issues, and it is to these that he speaks in the next three chapters. The situation just described is very real today in places where some members of a family owe allegiance to Christ, and others to other religions.

CARING FOR THE WEAK (8:1–13)

> 1 Now concerning things sacrificed to idols, we know that we all have knowledge. Knowledge makes arrogant, but love edifies.
> 2 If anyone supposes that he knows anything, he has not yet known as he ought to know;
> 3 but if anyone loves God, he is known by Him.
> 4 Therefore concerning the eating of things sacrificed to idols, we know that there is no such thing as an idol in the world, and that there is no God but one.
> 5 For even if there are so-called gods, whether in heaven or on earth, as indeed there are many gods and many lords,
> 6 yet for us there is *but* one God, the Father, from whom are all things and we *exist* for Him; and one Lord, Jesus Christ, by whom are all things, and we *exist* through Him.
> 7 However not all men have this knowledge; but some, being accustomed to the idol until now, eat *food* as if it were sacrificed to an idol; and their conscience being weak is defiled.
> 8 But food will not commend us to God; we are neither the worse if we do not eat, nor the better if we do eat.
> 9 But take care that this liberty of yours does not somehow become a stumbling block to the weak.

> 10 For if someone sees you, who have knowledge, dining in an idol's temple, will not his conscience, if he is weak, be strengthened to eat things sacrificed to idols?
>
> 11 For through your knowledge he who is weak is ruined, the brother for whose sake Christ died.
>
> 12 And so, by sinning against the brethren and wounding their conscience when it is weak, you sin against Christ.
>
> 13 Therefore, if food causes my brother to stumble, I will never eat meat again, so that I will not cause my brother to stumble.

Knowledge (8:1–3)

The opening phrase, with its similarity to 7:1, suggests that Paul is again drawing attention to a question that the Corinthians have asked him in their letter. The subject in question is "food sacrificed to idols"—that is, meat of animals which had been sacrificed to idols in pagan temples and was now ready to be eaten. Considering Paul's tone and answer, it would appear that some Corinthians felt that they were at liberty to eat such meat, based on their "knowledge" that idols were nothing. So, in answering the Corinthians' question, Paul begins by affirming what was common to him and the Corinthians, stating that "we know we all possess knowledge." Paul often uses the phrase "we know" in various letters, in passages where he is stating what he knows to be common ground between himself and his readers (cf. Rom 2:2; 3:19; 8:28; 1 Cor 7:14; 8:22; 2 Cor 5:1). However, Paul immediately proceeds to show that, while knowledge is important, it is insufficient to determine our relation to God and fellow human beings, particularly Christians. Instead, the opposite is actually true: "knowledge puffs up." The word here translated "puffs up," or literally "inflate," has already been used four times in this letter (see vv. 4, 6, 18, 19; 5:2), and it summarily expresses a major cause of the community's malaise. But, Paul says, "love builds up." Furthermore, Paul goes on to argue that real "knowledge" is not just to know God, but to be known by God. It is the person who loves God who truly knows God. Paul not only speaks of knowing God, but also of being known by God. Paul's assertions must have surprised the readers in two ways. First, Paul makes clear that knowing the truth about a particular issue was not enough. Rather, love was needed. The Corinthians surely needed to be reminded of this truth, given the high premium they obviously put upon knowledge of an intellectual rather than an ethical kind. No doubt they considered such knowledge to be the only arbiter in ethical problems.

Knowledge can lead to arrogance, and this settles nothing. It might establish the facts, but it does not establish the weaker believer. It might settle an argument, but it does not solve the problem of the weaker Christian. Second, whatever knowledge we have of God is due to God's loving initiative. Thus, it can be said that we love God only because God first loved us, and that we know God only because God first knew us. If people think that they have come into knowledge, and if they do not love fellow human beings, then the knowledge of the person, lacking love, is really incomplete.

There is only One God (8:4–6)

Paul returns to the problem of "food sacrificed to idols" in this verse. Still using the theme of knowledge. Paul now talks of what we know about God and the gods. His first assertion is that "an idol has no real existence" (v. 4). In other words, the gods that the idols represent are actually nonexistent. An idol was nothing but a piece of carved stone or wood, or shaped metal. Certainly it could not contaminate food. Paul seems to contradict himself in verse 5, as he asserts that there are many gods and lords. His point in the verse is that, although the gods specifically represented by the idols did not really exist, there were unseen beings behind the idols, a point that Paul would later expand on in chapter 10. Paul clarifies his position in verse 6. For Christians, there are no other beings in heaven or earth that may rightly be called God or Lord, apart from God the Father and the Lord Jesus Christ, but for others, such beings do exist. To have the true God, one must be in Christ. Creation owes its existence to God. As believers in Christ, we owe both our physical and spiritual existence to him. Paul next spoke of the Lord Jesus Christ as coequal with the Father. Before, he had used the phrase "from whom." Now Paul says "*through whom* are all things." Christ is the agent of all existence. Paul's point in this passage is clear. To some, now, as it was in Corinth, there were many gods and lords who commanded their loyalty, obedience, and service. Not so for the Christian. There is only one God who could demand total service and commitment, and only one Lord had made such service and commitment possible.

The second option shows why Paul interjected verse 6 into his argument about food sacrificed unto idols. Its purpose is to remind the Corinthian Christians (and us) that, whether weak or strong, we all owe our existence to God, and we are in a spiritual family through the grace of God in Christ. Therefore, as members of the same family, having the same Father and Savior, we must show concern for all family members, weak or strong. No one should do as he/she pleases or chooses.

Love before liberty (8:7–13)

In the preceding verses, Paul has just admitted the truth of the position maintained by some "knowledgeable" ones in Corinth that a false god has no real existence. But he now points out that not everyone possesses this knowledge. There were still some who thought that sacrificial meats have been contaminated by the gods represented by the idols. Although they probably believed with their minds that an idol is no god, they are yet unable to believe this truth from the depth of their hearts. As such, if they ate of meat sacrificed to idols, they thought that the mere act of consuming it amounted to participation in an idolatrous ritual. Such Christians cannot eat such meat without violating their conscience or, as Paul puts it, without their conscience being defiled. Eating is no proof that one is a good Christian; likewise, a refusal to eat is no proof that a Christian is spiritually deficient. Meat does not affect our standing with the Lord. For Paul, there was nothing either inherently good or evil in food itself. He knew the meaning of genuine Christian liberty. Just because we are free to eat does not mean we need to. There's no idea that freedom carries with it an imperative to act. Some people think that, because you're free to do something, that means you should do it. The result of that kind of thinking is that freedom itself becomes slavery. This is reminiscent of chapter 6, concerning the issue of sexual morality. Everything may be permissible, but not everything is helpful. In fact, one is no better off one way or the other, once a person understands his or her freedom of choice.

The strong Christians who possess the right knowledge about idols ought to "take heed" (v. 9, KJV). A person's sense of self-awareness is not sufficient to decide the course of action to take. Rather, Christians must be conscious of the effects of their actions on others. Those who are motivated by love for God and their fellow Christians will certainly not be indifferent to the harm their actions will cause others. The exercise of Christian liberty without Christian love can become a stumbling block to others. "Stumbling block" is used here in the sense of an offense. In the moral sense, it applies to what becomes an occasion for sin. What an indictment on twenty-first-century individualism.

Verse 10 shows the power of example. We are easily influenced by the decisions and actions of those around us. So, in verse 10, Paul describes how the thoughtless exercise of one's own liberty may lead to the downfall of a fellow Christian. If believers with weak consciences see those "with knowledge" sitting down to a meal in a heathen temple, they might be encouraged to eat meat consecrated to the heathen deity, even though they are unsure of the appropriateness of such a course. The result is tragic indeed. They have now a sense of having been disobedient to God. Having violated their consciences in one area of living, there is a breakdown of spiritual defenses, and they are exposed to violate his conscience in another area. Thus, he can suffer spiritual defeat and become useless to God (v. 11). That Paul is talking about eternal ruin is without a doubt. This is the import of the word translated as destroyed.

Verse 12 is a very serious verse, and one that believers need to consider afresh. An injury done to a child of God is an injury done to the Lord (cf. Acts 9:4). How grievous then is it to exercise one's personal liberty in a way that might cause a fellow Christian spiritual harm. Christians are so closely identified with Christ that to hurt one hurts the Savior. Hence, it is our responsibility to show an attitude of selfless concern for our brothers and sisters in Christ.

There are many areas of Christian life that cannot be classified as either absolute right or absolute wrong. Verse 13 speaks to such areas. However legitimate a thing may be, if under certain circumstances it becomes harmful to the members of a Christian, a Christian family, and to the cause of Christ, it must be avoided. The Christian must always ask themselves such questions as "Will my behavior build others up? Is love the controlling factor in my behavior or is it a desire to exert my personal rights? Am I willing to waive my rights for the sake of another?" Our conduct must not be determined solely on the basis of knowledge. It must be based on love.

QUESTIONS FOR PERSONAL REFLECTION

1. What is more important: to love or to know? Can we get by with just either of the two? Why or why not?
2. What should be a yardstick for the measurement of the believer's behavior—self or the community?

3. How far should we go in giving up our rights for the sake of others, particularly for those of weaker consciences?

4. If you were in a country or place where some Christians consider something to be wrong, what would you do if you did not consider the practice to be wrong?

5. How does love build up? What are the implications of this chapter for cross-cultural ministry?

6. How can we develop a greater love for others, a love that puts their spiritual good ahead of our personal liberty?

1 Corinthians 9:1–27

Christian Privileges: Use and Abuse

IN HIS DISCUSSION OF food sacrificed to idols in chapter 8, Paul has clearly articulated the need for selflessness among believers. But Paul's teaching about self-denial does not end with chapter 8; rather, it runs through the whole of chapter 9, showing other areas in which utter selflessness of the apostle was clearly visible. The chapter provides an example of the apostle Paul himself. He did not assert his rights.

Rights can be good. In Tom Clancy's "Hunt for Red October," Sam Neil's character was looking forward to defecting to America. In Russia, he had no choice in where to live except where the government told him to go. He needed permission in order to travel. The opposite is assumed in the United States and most of the Western world. Here, he could live where he wanted to and travel as freely and as often as he wished. Rights, rights, rights. Rights can be good. They can protect us. But just because we have a right to do something, should we do it? Perhaps Christians should be talking of privileges rather than rights. In 1 Corinthians 9, Paul gave the Corinthians, and we twenty-firs- century Christians, a model of how to and how not to use our Christian freedom and rights. What better example could Paul give but himself? So, he urges the Corinthians to consider his own example. His freedom was neither unrestricted nor uncontrolled. Rather, it was a freedom that was tempered with love. He begins the chapter with a series of rhetorical questions that demand positive answers. But chapter 9 goes beyond the question of how to enjoy freedom and exercise rights. It contains Paul's passionate defense of his apostleship, something that shows an intricate connection between the integrity of the messenger and his/her ministry. As Paul expands his statements regarding liberty and privilege, he introduces the subject of his apostleship. It is as though they had brought him before the bar of their own minds, and had rendered a verdict that he was a mere impostor. At the same time, the placing of Paul's apostolic defense in between the two discussions of meat offered to idols in chapters 8 and 10 suggests some connection between these two issues. It seems quite likely that Paul's apostolic authority was being further questioned on the grounds that he seemed inconsistent in his behavior, eating such food in gentile settings but declining it when among Jews.

PAUL'S APOSTOLIC PRIVILEGES (9:1–6)

> 1 Am I not free? Am I not an apostle? Have I not seen Jesus our Lord? Are you not my work in the Lord?
> 2 If to others I am not an apostle, at least I am to you; for you are the seal of my apostleship in the Lord.
> 3 My defense to those who examine me is this:
> 4 Do we not have a right to eat and drink?
> 5 Do we not have a right to take along a believing wife, even as the rest of the apostles and the brothers of the Lord and Cephas?
> 6 Or do only Barnabas and I not have a right to refrain from working?

Paul begins in an uncharacteristic manner, defending his authority as an apostle. He insists that he is free, holding that God-appointed position of an apostle. And even if other churches or Christians do not acknowledge Paul as an apostle, the Corinthians have to do so. Paul was the one who planted the church there. When a person graduates from an academic institution, he/she usually receives a piece of paper with some words on it, something that says that the bearer has fulfilled certain requirements and therefore is awarded a degree that is commensurate with the level of education. The significance of the paper lies in the seal of the institution, a special mark that shows that the authority of the institution is being used in awarding the degree. Thus, the fact that the Corinthians have been converted through Paul's ministry is an important factor for them to consider. God attested his ministry with their souls. As such, for the Corinthians to question the apostolic authority of Paul was to question the basis of their own existence as Christians.

Having defended his apostleship, Paul turns to his rights as an apostle. What were his rights and privileges? It included the right to be supported or maintained in material things by the churches, as well as the right to food and drink. That is, Barnabas and Paul had the right to expect the churches to relieve them of the necessity to labor with their hands by accepting responsibility for their material support. If this was their right, then it was also their right to forego that support. In Paul's time, itinerant missionaries known as Cynics prided themselves in being poor. In fact, poverty was seen as a mark of true apostleship. As such, by engaging in manual work, Paul opened himself up to a charge of not being an authentic apostle. Moreover, by striving to remain financially independent, Paul's behavior was altogether contrary to the culture of his day, particularly the Greco-Roman conventions of friendship and patronage. In Greco-Roman society, friendship between equals was closely bound up with the exchange of gifts. Moreover, philosophers and wandering missionaries frequently secured their livelihood by attaching themselves to a patron, a person of wealth and influence who gave them, as his clients, assistance and support in return for certain services. But Paul waived his rights. Second, Paul had the right to be married if he wished. One must note that Paul's refusal of support from the Corinthians was a matter of choice. It is not to be understood as an excuse for congregations not to support their ministers. Furthermore, although it was his right to be married, he chose to deny himself this right for the sake of being able to move freely among the churches without the responsibilities of marriage upon him in addition to the care of the churches in days of grave threat and difficulty.

BASIS OF SUPPORT AND PAUL'S CHOICE (9:7–12A)

7 Who at any time serves as a soldier at his own expense? Who plants a vineyard and does not eat the fruit of it? Or who tends a flock and does not use the milk of the flock?

8 I am not speaking these things according to human judgment, am I? Or does not the Law also say these things?

9 For it is written in the Law of Moses, "You shall not muzzle the ox while he is threshing." God is not concerned about oxen, is He?

10 Or is He speaking altogether for our sake? Yes, for our sake it was written, because the plowman ought to plow in hope, and the thresher *to thresh* in hope of sharing *the crops*.

11 If we sowed spiritual things in you, is it too much if we reap material things from you?

12 If others share the right over you, do we not more?

Once again, we must bear in mind the context of the chapter. Paul is telling the Corinthians that just because a person has freedom and "rights" does not always mean that a person should use or exploit those rights, especially if doing so will cause some harm or produce some adverse effects on others. Why did Paul feel that he was entitled to the support of the churches? First, it was customary for a person who rendered service to receive some kind of compensation for it. This was true of the soldier, the laborer in the vineyard, and the shepherd. Why then should the Christian worker who serves the spiritual interest of the churches be denied material support or compensation? Paul substantiates his right to support by citing the Scriptures (cf. Deut 25:4). If God was concerned about the care of oxen, do you think God is less concerned about ministers? Again, if the Corinthians gave material support to other servants of God, why should Paul not be entitled to support, since he planted the church? If an ox gets to eat some of the grain it is helping to grind, Christians should support the leaders who minister to and among them.

FREELY RECEIVED, FREELY GIVEN (9:12B–18)

> 12b Nevertheless, we did not use this right, but we endure all things so that we will cause no hindrance to the gospel of Christ.
>
> 13 Do you not know that those who perform sacred services eat the *food* of the temple, *and* those who attend regularly to the altar have their share from the altar?
>
> 14 So also the Lord directed those who proclaim the gospel to get their living from the gospel.
>
> 15 But I have used none of these things. And I am not writing these things so that it will be done so in my case; for it would be better for me to die than have any man make my boast an empty one.
>
> 16 For if I preach the gospel, I have nothing to boast of, for I am under compulsion; for woe is me if I do not preach the gospel.
>
> 17 For if I do this voluntarily, I have a reward; but if against my will, I have a stewardship entrusted to me.
>
> 18 What then is my reward? That, when I preach the gospel, I may offer the gospel without charge, so as not to make full use of my right in the gospel.

So why has Paul turned them down? Why has he refused and gone without, despite the hint that other apostles (probably Peter and Apollos) had accepted patronage? Paul is prepared to go without his rights because he does not want to let money get in the way of the gospel (v. 12). Paul preferred to suffer need rather than become burdensome to the Corinthians or to the other churches. To deny himself these rights was also his privilege. This is an unusual case of self-denial, something that, in principle, the churches of our day could well afford to see in the lives of their members and ministries. Paul wished that the Corinthians showed a similar concern not to put any hindrance in the way of fellow Christians with weaker faith (cf. 8:9, 13; 10:32). In the same way that it was said that John Wesley was "a man of only one book," it could be said that Paul was "a man of only one passion"—that is, the gospel of Christ. Paul was consumed by the gospel. The gospel was what he lived for. His credibility was bound with the gospel's.

In verse 14, he says that God has commanded that those who proclaim the gospel should be paid for it. He will insist on it for others, but not for himself. He'd rather support himself with his business as a tentmaker than ask the Corinthians for money and muddy the waters about his motivation. Paul's life was utterly consumed and motivated by proclaiming the good news from God about Jesus. He could not but do it. An obligation to proclaim it has been put on him. He is required to do it. If he proclaims it out of his own free desire, then his reward for doing so is that he makes it free of charge (v. 17–18). On the one hand, Paul is like every other Christian; he will say in 11:1 to imitate him as he imitates Christ. If we cannot be like him, then what's the point of imitating him? But on the other hand, Paul is utterly unique. For him, his conversion to Christianity and his commissioning to apostleship were one and the same event. But even in his unique role, and despite being an apostle, he will not make use of his rights, wanting to make it easier for people to believe, not harder.

ALL THINGS TO ALL PEOPLE (9:19–23)

> 19 For though I am free from all *men*, I have made myself a slave to all, so that I may win more.
>
> 20 To the Jews I became as a Jew, so that I might win Jews; to those who are under the Law, as under the Law though not being myself under the Law, so that I might win those who are under the Law;
>
> 21 to those who are without law, as without law, though not being without the law of God but under the law of Christ, so that I might win those who are without law.

> 22 To the weak I became weak, that I might win the weak; I have become all things to all men, so that I may by all means save some.
> 23 I do all things for the sake of the gospel, so that I may become a fellow partaker of it.

Paul started and concluded the previous paragraph on the same note. He had personally and willingly renounced his apostolic rights for the sake of the gospel. He was probably aware that his conduct has appeared to some to be inconsistent and contradictory, and so he has done his utmost to show that the apparent inconsistency of his conduct is solely due to his one overruling aim, to be the most effective witness to the gospel that he can possibly be. Now he sees an opportunity to show how other apparent inconsistencies in the pattern of his life have the same explanation. As he is to explain in the following chapter (10:23–33), it is his practice to eat or not eat marketplace food, depending on the situation. This stance probably laid him open to the charge of inconsistency. Paul's defense is, in essence, that people cannot be evangelized at arm's length. To bring the gospel home to men and women and win them to Christ's allegiance, the preacher must get alongside them. Paul is willing to shed every vestige of his inherited Jewish lifestyle and adopt the lifestyle of anyone at all, or, on the other hand, to resume Jewish manners and customs, in order to reach out to others. Such is Paul's passion for the gospel.

Paul's refusal to exercise his right to material support is part of his broader understanding of his mission. Paul is not one thing while pretending to be another. Paul is free from their categories. He is free to act in the most helpful way in each individual setting. Would Paul have eaten pork in the presence of a Moslem while trying to win him to Christ, or would he have eaten non-kosher food (bacon burger) in front of a Jew while he tells him that Jesus loves him? Probably not. He will not eat meat from the pagan temples with those who are still in awe of idols as gods. Paul's primary allegiance was to Christ, and his identity is wrapped up with being in Christ. His particular actions with any group will not betray Jesus. But he will act in ways that make it easier, not harder, for others to come to faith in Jesus. And he does not pretend that he does not act differently with different groups. This is Paul as the caring pastor and sensitive evangelist. He will not sin; he will not become like a liar to the liars, or a murderer to the murderers. But he will act appropriately for the needs of each group. As he says in verse 22, he has become all things to all people, that he might save some. Paul's burning desire is to see people be saved, not to stand proudly on his rights. He will gladly not insist on them if it helps others to believe. Paul is driven by principles—not the principle of exercising his rights, but the salvation of others. Paul's determination is to be governed in everything he does by the gospel, not simply in order to share it with others, but in order to share with them in its blessings. For Paul, his rights in the gospel are a wonderful, God-given blessing, but one he will gladly go without for the sake of others. He is not possessive. Paul is no hypocrite. Neither is he a legalistic rights lawyer. What is always there is his love for God, his desire for others to hear, and his sensitivities to the needs of each group. Paul tempers his freedom and rights with love.

THE NEED FOR DISCIPLINE (9:24–27)

> 24 Do you not know that those who run in a race all run, but *only* one receives the prize? Run in such a way that you may win.
> 25 Everyone who competes in the games exercises self-control in all things. They then *do it* to receive a perishable wreath, but we an imperishable.
> 26 Therefore I run in such a way, as not without aim; I box in such a way, as not beating the air;
> 27 but I discipline my body and make it my slave, so that, after I have preached to others, I myself will not be disqualified.

In these last three verses, Paul is saying that although he is free, he lives a disciplined life. Paul's primary concern in this paragraph is not to justify his personal practice, but to warn the Corinthians against presumption, by way of preparation for the following chapter. Like runners in a marathon or Olympic gymnasts, Paul goes about his mission with iron discipline. Every athlete goes into strict training. Before they could compete in the Isthmian Games (held outside Corinth), athletes had to undergo ten months of strict training. They did it to win a fading garland, but we, to win a garland that never fades. In other words, the Christian life calls for total commitment. The garland that never fades is eternal life. A runner who stops to enjoy the view will not win the race.

Paul is single-minded in his life. He is prepared to go without, not insisting on his rights, if that will help him to achieve his mission. Paul is running to win. He is under no illusions about how hard it will be, being a slave to all; conforming rather than insisting on his rights; going without,

1 CORINTHIANS

so that others gain from the gospel. It is hard work. But if one of the revered and influential apostles can do this, so can the Corinthians. He is giving them a gentle nudge, urging them to mimic him. Rather than strongly insisting on their way because it is their right, they should try tempering their freedom and rights with love. Christian maturity consists not of knowing your rights and freedoms, but on giving them up for others. One must be careful not to press the analogy here. The Christian life is not a race in which only the top competitor wins a prize and all the others get nothing, however hard they may have striven. There are two principles from Paul's example. Paul usually tempers his freedom and gives up his rights to win people for Christ. And he tempers his freedom and gives up his rights as an act of love towards other Christians.

1. Freedom to win others for Christ

Paul's primary application is about winning people for Christ. He wants to make it as easy as possible for people to become Christians, and refuses to let his own rights become an impediment for them. In verses 12 and 22, Paul opens a window into his heart for others. What drives him, what moves him to give up his rights, is his desire to see people become Christians. Whenever he came across a people group or a town, Paul saw people in need of the gospel; people for whom he would be willing to give up his rights if it would make it easier for them to come to faith. We need to ask ourselves what rights we have as a church or as a group of individuals that we cling to and protect when they can actually get in the way of people to come to Jesus? We are within our rights to do them, but if the apostle Paul could refuse his rights, so can we, if it will help others to faith. And what Paul did and calls us to is nothing less than the example of Jesus himself. In Philippians 2, Paul calls the church to consider Jesus. If anyone had rights it was he, God himself, and yet he did not stand on his rights, but became a servant for our sake. He took on the role of a servant. God humbled himself, even to the point of death. If one no less than Jesus can do this for our sake, we can do it so others can benefit from his death and resurrection for us.

2. Freedom to love other Christians

Paul's other concern is about using freedom and overlooking rights for the sake of other Christians. This is especially hard for many of us. Our society treasures individualism. I'll fight to protect my right to do something even at the cost of hurting others. It is impossible to be a lone wolf Christian. Paul's view is that to be a Christian means being part of a church. As the Yoruba proverb goes, "Agabajo owo la fi nsoya, ese girigiri lo nyena," meaning that "a tree does not make a forest." That communal aspect of being a Christian is why Paul's example of how to handle maturely Christian freedom and rights is so important. It is only in the context of a community that the exercise of our rights and freedom becomes so important. Going to church does not save a person. But the church is the body of saved people. And Paul's appeal is for Christians to behave in a mature loving way together.

QUESTIONS FOR PERSONAL REFLECTION

1. When should Christians in general, and ministers in particular, be willing to give up their rights?
2. What is true Christian freedom?
3. Why is it crucial to provide financial support for ministers?
4. What does it mean to be "all things to all people," and what pitfalls are to be avoided?
5. What are the evidences of success that mark our service for Christ?

1 Corinthians 10:1–33

Flee from Idolatry

IN CHAPTERS 8 AND 9, Paul had focused on the question of meats offered to idols. This issue is first raised in chapter 8. There Paul indicates that the Corinthians' right to eat meat, based on their "knowledge," is to be set aside for the sake of their "weaker" brethren. To insist on exercising their rights by eating such meat to the detriment of their fellow believers is contrary to love. Moving on, in chapter 9, Paul contrasts his personal example about attitudes and actions with those who insist on eating these meats. Without mincing words, he demonstrates his right to "eat and drink" at the expense of the brethren to whom he ministers. He does so by drawing support from the Old Testament law, everyday living, from the practice of his fellow apostles, and from the teaching of our Lord. Nevertheless, Paul argues that, in spite of his undeniable right to "eat and drink" at the expense of others, he forgoes his personal right and liberty so that his ministry of the gospel will be enhanced. What an irony! While the Corinthians argued about exercising a "right" that is wrong and no right at all, Paul sets aside an incontestable "right." Paul cast his discussion in a wider historical and scriptural context: the Exodus story. For Paul, the problem of the Corinthians was nothing unusual. It simply mirrored the problem of the ancient Israelites when they left Egypt for the promised land of Canaan. They were plagued with the problem of self-indulgence and instant gratification. It is important to note that the problems that the twenty-first-century Christian faces are in many ways similar to those which the Israelites or the Corinthians faced.

FLEE FROM IDOLATRY

THE DANGER OF IDOLATRY (10:1–13)

> 1 For I do not want you to be unaware, brethren, that our fathers were all under the cloud and all passed through the sea;
> 2 and all were baptized into Moses in the cloud and in the sea;
> 3 and all ate the same spiritual food;
> 4 and all drank the same spiritual drink, for they were drinking from a spiritual rock which followed them; and the rock was Christ.
> 5 Nevertheless, with most of them God was not well-pleased; for they were laid low in the wilderness.
> 6 Now these things happened as examples for us, so that we would not crave evil things as they also craved.
> 7 Do not be idolaters, as some of them were; as it is written, "The people sat down to eat and drink, and stood up to play."
> 8 Nor let us act immorally, as some of them did, and twenty-three thousand fell in one day.
> 9 Nor let us try the Lord, as some of them did, and were destroyed by the serpents.
> 10 Nor grumble, as some of them did, and were destroyed by the destroyer.
> 11 Now these things happened to them as an example, and they were written for our instruction, upon whom the ends of the ages have come.
> 12 Therefore let him who thinks he stands take heed that he does not fall.
> 13 No temptation has overtaken you but such as is common to man; and God is faithful, who will not allow you to be tempted beyond what you are able, but with the temptation will provide the way of escape also, so that you will be able to endure it.

Blessed but Disqualified (10:1–5)

Paul continues with the theme he has introduced in 9:24–27, in which he emphasizes the danger of disqualification. In doing so, he points to the example of the ancient Israelites who, although they experienced many miracles and enjoyed many blessings and special privileges, failed to enter the promised land of Canaan. Instead, many of them perished in the wilderness. Paul enumerates the Israelites' blessings as follows.

1. They all were under the cloud and all passed through the Red Sea. In the Exodus story, Israel was not only miraculously delivered, but also

was guided by God in its journey through the wilderness by means of the pillar of cloud by day and the pillar of fire by night. Israel's experience in the exodus from Egypt prefigures that of the Corinthians becoming Christians.

2. They were all baptized unto Moses. The point of Paul's comparison is to show that the Israelites had been baptized into Moses in the same manner that the Corinthians have been baptized into Christ. Hence, Paul compares the situation of the Corinthians with that of the Israelites in which baptism conveys identification with someone. The Israelites were identified with Moses, just as the Corinthians were identified with Christ.

3. They all ate the same spiritual food and the same spiritual drink. In referring to the manna (Exod 16:12–35) and the water from the rock (Exod 17:6; Num 20:11) as spiritual, Paul does not suggest that the food and drink were not physical and ordinary. Nevertheless, they have spiritual signification. They were not only miraculously provided, but also they were provided by the Spirit, and as such, had spiritual power for God's people. Paul was emphatic as he says, "the Rock was Christ." Thus, he symbolically connected Christ with the water-giving rock in the wilderness. The point of Paul's comparison comes up in verse 5: "Nevertheless, God was not pleased with most of them, and they were struck down in the wilderness."

God supernaturally met all the needs of all the Israelites during their wanderings in the wilderness. He divinely provided for their salvation, their protection, and their guidance. God provided for the food and water that these Israelites required while in the wilderness. Yet in spite of all these divine provisions, the Israelites failed to enter into the land. One cannot but notice the use of "all" five times in the passage. Many left Egypt; all partook of divine blessings and privileges; only two entered the promised land. The lesson is clear: Divine blessings and privileges are not guarantees against disqualification if one chooses to live contrary to God's words. No one can ever say that they failed to finish the race because they were not adequately provided for. Those who failed to enter into the promised land are those who failed not only to appreciate but also to appropriate God's provisions. More than this, those who failed to enter into the promised land were those who lacked self-discipline, and who fell due to their self-indulgence.

Flee from Idolatry

Israel's History—For Our sakes (10:6–10)

In verses 6–10, Paul identifies those specific sins which plagued the ancient Israelites, resulting in their failure to please God and to possess the land of Canaan. Each of these failures is a sin of self-indulgence, and each points to a sin that is prominent in the Corinthian Church of Paul's day, as well as in our church today. In allowing these things to happen, God had in mind not only that generation, but our own. What were their problems? The answer lies in Paul's exhortations to the Corinthians.

1. Paul exhorts the Corinthians not to become idolaters, alluding to the story of the golden calf in Exodus 32:6. This is a command that directly relates to the problem addressed by Paul in chapters 8–10. The ancient Israelites ate in the presence of the golden calf. With this, Paul shows a direct parallel between the misconduct of the Corinthians and the eating of cultic meals in the idol's presence in Corinth. The verb underlying "play" quite possibly carries overtones of sexual play.

2. The Corinthians were to shun sexual immorality, something that led to the destruction of twenty-three thousand Israelites in one day. This command dovetails with Paul's earlier discussion in 1 Corinthians 5:1–13 and 6:12–20 concerning sexual immorality among the Corinthians. In those passages, as we have previously noted, Paul did not spare the rod, but seriously castigated the Corinthians because of the behavioral aberrations. The story in Numbers 25:1–9 to which Paul alludes is particularly relevant to the Corinthians. In that instance, the plague that God sent on Israel was due to sexual immorality that was associated with idolatry.

3. In verse 9, Paul warns the Corinthians against putting the Lord to the test as the Israelites did and were bitten to death by fiery serpents. Paul alludes to the story in Numbers 21:4–9 so as to show the self-indulgence of the Corinthians. Like the Israelites of old, they had cravings that could not be easily satisfied. They rejected the manna due to their lack of satisfaction with God's provision. They wanted "something else," thus tempting God.

4. Finally, Paul warns the Corinthians against their incessant complaints and grumbles, something that characterized the Israelites. They seized every opportunity to grumble against God and Moses. It is also likely that, just as the Israelites grumbled against Moses, so the Corinthians

have been grumbling against Paul about leadership and his teaching which they did not like much. Thus, the Corinthians, like the Israelites, grumbled against God. Although Paul was probably alluding to Numbers 14:1–38, the language about the "destroyer" is borrowed from Exodus 12:23. In verse 10, Paul repeats what he said in verse 6 that the experience of the Israelites in the wilderness happened for "our benefit." They were, in a sense, symbolic and recorded as a warning for Paul's day and ours.

Watch, Trust, and Flee (10:12–13)

> 12 Therefore let him who thinks he stands take heed that he does not fall.
>
> 13 No temptation has overtaken you but such as is common to man; and God is faithful, who will not allow you to be tempted beyond what you are able, but with the temptation will provide the way of escape also, so that you will be able to endure it.

The Corinthians must learn from the example of the Israelites lest they suffer the same fate. They must avoid self-confidence, self-reliance, and complacency. Presuming upon God's grace is a great danger that believers must avoid. Therefore, Paul writes, "so if you think you are standing, watch out that you do not fall." How appropriate are the words of the song:

> *Christian seek not yet repose*
> *Cast thy dreams of ease away*
> *You are in the midst of foes*
> *Watch and pray*

Paul goes on to show that God's power is available to keep them standing. Therefore they must trust. Yet it is not Paul's intention to leave his hearers in a state of fear and trembling, and so verse 13 marks a sudden switch of mood. Having demolished false self-reliance, Paul now seeks to build up proper confidence; confidence that is not in themselves, but in God, who will not allow them to be overwhelmed by trial. God is faithful and will not let you be tested beyond your powers, but when the test comes, he will at the same time provide a way out and so enable you to endure.

INCOMPATIBILITY OF IDOLS
WITH CHRISTIAN COMMUNION (10:14–22)

> 14 Therefore, my beloved, flee from idolatry.
> 15 I speak as to wise men; you judge what I say.
> 16 Is not the cup of blessing which we bless a sharing in the blood of Christ? Is not the bread which we break a sharing in the body of Christ?
> 17 Since there is one bread, we who are many are one body; for we all partake of the one bread.
> 18 Look at the nation Israel; are not those who eat the sacrifices sharers in the altar?
> 19 What do I mean then? That a thing sacrificed to idols is anything, or that an idol is anything?
> 20 *No*, but *I say* that the things which the Gentiles sacrifice, they sacrifice to demons and not to God; and I do not want you to become sharers in demons.
> 21 You cannot drink the cup of the Lord and the cup of demons; you cannot partake of the table of the Lord and the table of demons.
> 22 Or do we provoke the Lord to jealousy? We are not stronger than He, are we?

Paul appeals to the Corinthians as dear friends. His exhortation is an urgent one; that the Corinthians flee immediately from idolatry, having just demonstrated the awful consequences of idolatry as seen in the story of Israel. History records that Greeks and Romans had integrated the worship of their pagan gods into the entire fabric of their national and domestic life. Small altars were erected in homes, and statutes were placed in gardens. The temple ceremonies, state occasions, festival events, and even family gatherings involved the sacrifices of animals to the pagan gods (idols) of the day. These things posed serious problems for the Christians in Corinth. Suppose a family gathered together in what we call a family reunion, an occasion that could take place either at home, in one of the rooms of the temple, or in the temple court. An offering would be made to the gods, and part of the offering would be prepared for the reunion. What should the Christian do? To eat or not to eat becomes a crucial question. Should the Christian eat meats that were sacrificed to idols, having been sacrificed by their priests? Virtually all of the meat available for purchase came from animals that had been offered on the altar of a pagan god. The Christian is now in "between a rock and a hard place." Thus, Paul appeals to their common sense.

Running through the whole chapter is this concern with idolatry in Corinth (vv. 7, 14, 19, 28). The pagan sacrifices to idols in Corinth were a tough issue for the church. Does a believer eat the meat used in such sacrifices when it is resold in the market? Does one go to dinner in a person's house when they might use such meat? Could one participate in the ceremonies themselves? Idolatry was not merely a theoretical issue in Corinth. It was a real-life everyday problem. And it still is today, though the idols and the sacrifices have changed. After urging the Corinthians to flee from idolatry, Paul moves on to discuss the observance of the Lord's Supper, focusing on participation in the body and blood of Jesus Christ. When partaking of the Lord's Supper, believers enter into a communal relationship with others in their fellowship. Moving from this understanding of fellowship, Paul discusses unity and fellowship among individual Christians. Though there may be many members of a group, there is one congregation. Just as all believers partake in the one bread of communion, all participate in the one body of Christ. Emphasis is placed on Christian unity by the repetition of the word "one." Christians must recognize this unity in their fellowship with Christ and with one another. The main point of verse 16 is clear: participation in the Lord's Supper brings about a particular bond with Christ. It is thus designed to lead to verses 20–22, in which Paul will assert that participation in pagan sacrifices brings about a particular bond with demons, and then draw the conclusion that these two bonds are incompatible.

Beginning from verse 18, Paul develops the warning first sounded in verse 14. He has stressed the reality of the participation brought about in the Lord's Supper—that is, participation in the body and blood of Christ with others. Now he is to argue that participation in any cultic meal is not a harmless act, but one that relates the worshipers, to their detriment, to some reality behind the rite. Evidently, the Corinthians have been justifying their participation in pagan cultic meals on the grounds that an idol has no real existence, so that any meat offered to an idol is no more than mere meat (v. 19). But Paul insists that any food offered on a pagan altar is not offered to any being worthy of the name of God, but this does not mean that the worshipers are not in touch with anything at all. On the contrary, they become partners with demons—for Paul, an intolerable state of affairs. He is here echoing a belief expressed in a number of Old Testament passages that pagan sacrifices, as well as the sacrifices offered to pagan gods by apostate Jews, are in fact offered to demons (see especially Deut 32:17). It follows that the two forms of sacred meals, the Lord's Supper and the pagan cultic meal, are incompatible. You cannot drink the cup of the Lord and the cup of demons. You cannot partake of the Lord's table and the table of demons.

To do otherwise would be to provoke the Lord, to put him to the test of a trial of strength. It is clear from 8:9–12 that the dominant group in Corinth thought of themselves not only as enlightened, mature, and spiritual, but also as strong, in contrast to other Christians who were, in their eyes, unenlightened, immature, unspiritual, and weak. "Strong you may be," Paul says to them, "but you are surely not so foolhardy as to take on God." This passage raises two problems in particular: one historical, and the other having to do with the meaning of the passage for today.

First, what is the relation between the practices Paul is condemning here and the practice he condemns in chapter 8? We have already discussed this question in the introduction to 8:1—11:1; in chapter 8, Paul is primarily concerned with the problem presented by the meat per se—that is, the problem of whether or not Christians might eat meat that had passed through a pagan temple. While there is a reference at 8:10 to someone who might be seen participating in a meal in a temple, Paul seems to have in mind an occasion which is primarily a social event. In the present passage, on the other hand, he is talking about meals within temple precincts, which have a distinct religious focus. In 10:23—11:1, however, he reverts to the question of the propriety of eating the meat.

USE OF CHRISTIAN FREEDOM FOR THE SAKE OF OTHERS (10:23–11:1)

> 23 All things are lawful, but not all things are profitable. All things are lawful, but not all things edify.
>
> 24 Let no one seek his own *good*, but that of his neighbor.
>
> 25 Eat anything that is sold in the meat market without asking questions for conscience's sake;
>
> 26 for the earth is the Lord's, and all it contains.
>
> 27 If one of the unbelievers invites you and you want to go, eat anything that is set before you without asking questions for conscience' sake.

> 28 But if anyone says to you, "This is meat sacrificed to idols," do not eat *it*, for the sake of the one who informed *you*, and for conscience' sake;
>
> 29 I mean not your own conscience, but the other *man's*; for why is my freedom judged by another's conscience?
>
> 30 If I partake with thankfulness, why am I slandered concerning that for which I give thanks?
>
> 31 Whether, then, you eat or drink or whatever you do, do all to the glory of God.
>
> 32 Give no offense either to Jews or to Greeks or to the church of God;
>
> 33 just as I also please all men in all things, not seeking my own profit but the *profit* of the many, so that they may be saved.
>
> 1 Be imitators of me, just as I also am of Christ.

Paul now begins to draw to a conclusion the long discussion on meat offered to idols that he began in chapter 8. As he does so, he engages still more intensively with the Corinthian standpoint. The opening words of verse 23 are identical with the opening words of 6:12, apart from the omission of one word. The intent of Paul's correction of the Corinthian position here is very much in the spirit of chapter 8. There he qualifies their claim to have knowledge by affirming the priority of love. Here he qualifies their claim to be free by urging that each look after the interests of others, not their own, and in this way build up the community. This is, in fact, the dominant emphasis of the whole passage, that the Christian's conduct must always be determined by consideration for the neighbor's spiritual welfare, the neighbor's conscience, so that the church may be built up (cf. vv. 28, 32).

Out of consideration for the neighbor, the Christian will be willing to set aside his or her freedom, but that freedom is still a reality, and Paul now strongly affirms it. You may eat anything sold in the meat market without raising questions of conscience. For Paul, meat in itself is harmless whatever its immediate origin, since the earth is the Lord's and all that is in it (v. 26). Therefore, whenever the Corinthians are invited to the home of a non-Christian for a meal, they are to eat whatever is put before them, without raising questions of conscience. In other words, they may eat it with a perfectly clear conscience (v. 27). Yet, if on such an occasion somebody should say "This food has been offered in sacrifice," then they are not to eat it, out of consideration for the other person and his conscience (v. 28). On the other hand, how could you claim to be honoring God by acting in a way that gave offense to Jews or Greeks or to the church of God?

"Giving offense" here clearly means something more serious than hurting someone's feelings. It means acting in a way that would make it difficult for another person either to hear the gospel or to remain a believer.

The injunction to be careful to give no offense should not be understood as something additional to the preceding injunction to do everything to the glory of God, but rather as part of its explication. This is something that Paul has to impress upon the Corinthians again and again, that the service of God and the service of others are inextricably associated. To seal the argument, Paul cites his own behavior, as being one who seeks to live by the rule he has just stated. Consideration for his neighbor's spiritual welfare is his constant concern, the good of the many rather than his own good.

QUESTIONS FOR PERSONAL REFLECTION

1. What are the significant lessons to learn from the story of the Israelites? What sins did Israel commit? What can Christians learn from their ordeal in the wilderness?
2. What is the promise of God available to the Christian in times of temptation? In what way do you think that this promise may be abused?
3. Are there things that cannot be done to the glory of God? Name some of them.
4. How important is the consideration for the spiritual welfare of others in determining a specific course of actions? Does not this make us lose our liberty as individuals?
5. What does a Christian whose other extended family members belong to other religions do when they celebrate their festivals with meat sacrificed unto idols?

1 Corinthians 11:1–34

Your Supper or the Lord's Supper?

THE LORD'S SUPPER IS the central focus of this particular passage. Paul reminded the Corinthians that when they gather together to share in a communal meal at the Lord's holy table, it is not the table of any particular patron. Behaviors or practices that exclude members of the congregation from partaking in the Lord's Supper because of their social status are a serious hindrance to establishing authentic Christian community. Paul begins by talking about the church as the body of Christ. The section ends in the same manner, discussing the Lord's Supper in relation to Christ's body. Discerning the Lord's body correctly requires right actions and practices. Also, believers must aim for unity among one another to interpret correctly and participate in the communion meal. Collectively, the church must examine herself as the Lord's Supper is administered.

Paul's Example (11:1)

> 1 Be imitators of me, as I am of Christ.

The verse emphasizes the power of example. The Corinthian Christians needed good examples, and Paul was willing to be one. How few today are willing to say what Paul said! Instead, because of compromise and ungodliness, we are quick to say, "Do not look at me, look at Jesus." While it is true that we must all ultimately look to Jesus, every one of us should be an example to others. However, Paul was quick to add that he was to be followed as he, in turn, followed Christ. This also sets a limit and a direction on the way we imitate others. Just as I also imitate Christ has the idea of "follow me as much as you see me following Jesus." Paul knew he was following Jesus, so he did not hesitate to tell the Corinthian Christians to imitate his walk with the Lord.

HEAD COVERING (11:2–16)

> 2 Now I praise you because you remember me in everything and hold firmly to the traditions, just as I delivered them to you.
>
> 3 But I want you to understand that Christ is the head of every man, and the man is the head of a woman, and God is the head of Christ.
>
> 4 Every man who has *something* on his head while praying or prophesying disgraces his head.
>
> 5 But every woman who has her head uncovered while praying or prophesying disgraces her head, for she is one and the same as the woman whose head is shaved.
>
> 6 For if a woman does not cover her head, let her also have her hair cut off; but if it is disgraceful for a woman to have her hair cut off or her head shaved, let her cover her head.
>
> 7 For a man ought not to have his head covered, since he is the image and glory of God; but the woman is the glory of man.
>
> 8 For man does not originate from woman, but woman from man;
>
> 9 for indeed man was not created for the woman's sake, but woman for the man's sake.
>
> 10 Therefore the woman ought to have *a symbol of* authority on her head, because of the angels.
>
> 11 However, in the Lord, neither is woman independent of man, nor is man independent of woman.
>
> 12 For as the woman originates from the man, so also the man *has his birth* through the woman; and all things originate from God.
>
> 13 Judge for yourselves: is it proper for a woman to pray to God *with her head* uncovered?
>
> 14 Does not even nature itself teach you that if a man has long hair, it is a dishonor to him,
>
> 15 but if a woman has long hair, it is a glory to her? For her hair is given to her for a covering.
>
> 16 But if one is inclined to be contentious, we have no other practice, nor have the churches of God.

When discussing 1 Corinthians 11:2–16, most interpreters have focused on the issues of authority and veils. As important as those may be, such discussions miss the whole point of the argument to which both the question of veil and authority are only incidental. Paul's argument in this section is part of his broader discussion on Christian worship that runs through chapters 11–14. In particular, the verses must be linked to the context of the Lord's Supper that immediately follows. Moreover, the failure to see the section in its sociocultural context continues to generate controversies in many places around the world, particularly in Africa, a largely patriarchal society. Contrary to the custom of their day, some Corinthian women were praying and prophesying with their head unbound, while some men, likewise engaged, wore their hair long. So, the problems in this section seemed to have revolved around head covering and hairstyles. Why the Corinthians decided to abandon the customs remains unclear. It has been suggested that in that day, prostitutes, as a demonstration of their freedom of not being under a husband's authority, not only wore their hair cut short, but also without any covering over their head. Regardless of the Corinthians' motivation, Paul repudiates the abandonment of the prevalent custom of the day, which was head covering and long hair for women, and no head covering and short hair for men.

Paul's position is predicated on three arguments. First is the cultural practice of that day. Women who pray or prophesy without a head covering dishonor their head, while men who transgress the hair etiquette dishonor Christ (vv. 4–6). Paul further argues that it is a shame. Why? It blurs the proper male/female relationship. Paul's second argument is based on the creation account of Genesis 2. Paul explains his assertion that the woman reflects the glory of man because she is formed from him. Hence, a woman should avoid anything that dishonors a man. In other words, she must keep her hair bound. Paul's statement in verse 10 is enigmatic. Lest Paul's words be misunderstood as a call for the absolute subordination of women, he affirms male/female equality and mutual interdependence in verses 11 and 12. However, such equality is not to lead to the abandonment of the social norms or the abolition of gender differences. Paul's third and final argument for head covering is in verse 13–16. He argues from nature.

THE LORD'S SUPPER (11:17–34)

1. The Problem at Corinth and Paul's Rebuke (11:17–22)

> 17 But in giving this instruction, I do not praise you, because you come together not for the better but for the worse.
>
> 18 For, in the first place, when you come together as a church, I hear that divisions exist among you; and in part I believe it.
>
> 19 For there must also be factions among you, so that those who are approved may become evident among you.
>
> 20 Therefore when you meet together, it is not to eat the Lord's Supper,
>
> 21 for in your eating each one takes his own supper first; and one is hungry and another is drunk.
>
> 22 What! Do you not have houses in which to eat and drink? Or do you despise the church of God and shame those who have nothing? What shall I say to you? Shall I praise you? In this I will not praise you.

The main concern here is participation in the Lord's Supper. If you were able to witness the Corinthian Church's observance of the Lord's Supper, you just might wonder if any Christians were present, for the disorders at the celebration were shocking. The Corinthian Church was certainly not engaging in positive practices, but rather acting for the worse. They have turned the Lord's Supper into an occasion for drunkenness and gluttony. The whole shameful event rendered a proper observance of the Lord's Supper impossible (v. 20).

Paul also highlights the problem of division among the Corinthians, particularly as it related to their social status. Have you ever felt despised and unwelcome at feasts or at meals? If so, you are not alone. In Greco-Roman society, people were usually seated according to socioeconomic status at meal tables. The rich had contempt for the poor and despised them even though they were in the same community. Paul also highlights the problem of selfishness in the congregation. So, when Paul says that each of you goes ahead without waiting for anybody else, he reveals how selfish and self-centered they had become. Some of the Corinthians were just diving in without waiting, even taking all the food for themselves. Some, as a result, were going hungry, while others were even getting drunk. What a selfish disgrace! Paul condemns such behavior. The Lord's Supper is an event that should be accessible to all social levels. By shaming those less fortunate in the community, the Corinthian Church, in fact, shames herself. Rather than honoring the body of Christ, the Corinthians brought reproach to the church.

2. Paul's Rehearsal of the Lord's Supper (11:23–26)

> 23 For I received from the Lord that which I also delivered to you, that the Lord Jesus in the night in which He was betrayed took bread;
> 24 and when He had given thanks, He broke it and said, "This is My body, which is for you; do this in remembrance of Me."
> 25 In the same way *He took* the cup also after supper, saying, "This cup is the new covenant in My blood; do this, as often as you drink *it*, in remembrance of Me."
> 26 For as often as you eat this bread and drink the cup, you proclaim the Lord's death until He comes.

Why is the Lord's Supper so significant? Why must it be done right? Paul continues his correction of the Corinthians' degradation of the Lord's Supper by showing them its true meaning. It is a special meal, Paul says, because of its historical roots. We remember that the Last Supper was actually a Passover meal, when Jesus, together with the disciples, according to Jewish traditions, celebrated the remembrance of Israel's deliverance from Egypt to the promised land, beginning in the book of Exodus. The breaking of bread and the drinking of wine were important parts of the Passover celebration. Jesus took these important pictures and reminders of Israel's deliverance from Egypt and added to them the meanings connected with his own death on the cross for us. As such we must be careful not to minimize the significance of the Lord's Supper by reducing it to a mere symbol. The celebration of the Lord's Supper is grounded in Jesus' final meal with his disciples. It is a tradition that came straight from the Lord. Thus, Paul is reminding the Corinthians that the supper that they were abusing was rooted in the words and actions of Christ on the night of his betrayal, something that demands that they take time to reflect the intense pathos of that event. For Paul, the supper is not only rooted in Christ's words, but also his actions.

In discussing the Lord's Supper, Paul puts the emphasis on remembering Jesus, on what he said about the meaning of his own death for us. They are powerful pictures to partake of, to enter into, as we see the Lord's table as the new Passover. Christ's death, which is celebrated in the Lord's Supper, established the new covenant between God and his people—a covenant that promises forgiveness for every sinner that repents. The phrase, "new testament," or "new covenant" is an echo of Jeremiah 31:31. Christ shows his solidarity and continuity of the church with the traditions of Israel and their hopeful expectations. To be in covenant relationship with God is to belong to a covenant people that are bound together by responsibilities to God as well as one another. The sharing of the meal is a visible demonstration of the character of the covenant. Because of what Jesus did on the cross, we can have a new covenant relationship with God.

Furthermore, the Lord's Supper is of crucial importance because of its confessional nature. It proclaims the Lord's death until he comes. Participation in the Lord's Supper becomes a visible proclamation of the message of the Church; Christ's death and resurrection (vv. 25–26).

3. Unintended Consequences (11:27–34)

> 27 Therefore whoever eats the bread or drinks the cup of the Lord in an unworthy manner shall be guilty of the body and the blood of the Lord.
>
> 28 But a man must examine himself, and in so doing he is to eat of the bread and drink of the cup.
>
> 29 For he who eats and drinks, eats and drinks judgment to himself if he does not judge the body rightly.
>
> 30 For this reason many among you are weak and sick, and a number sleep.
>
> 31 But if we judged ourselves rightly, we would not be judged.
>
> 32 But when we are judged, we are disciplined by the Lord so that we will not be condemned along with the world.
>
> 33 So then, my brethren, when you come together to eat, wait for one another.
>
> 34 If anyone is hungry, let him eat at home, so that you will not come together for judgment. The remaining matters I will arrange when I come.

Paul has now set forth the meaning of the Lord's Supper. Now he defines the "worthy" manner in which it should be observed. Paul's admonition takes a very solemn tone in these verses. Their abuse of the Eucharist (a potential fellowship with the Risen Christ and remembrance of the earthly Jesus) was serious and had grave negative consequences. Hence Paul says, "For this reason, many are weak and sick among you, and many sleep . . . But if anyone is hungry, let him eat at home, lest you come together for judgment.

And the rest I will set in order when I come?" (vv. 30, 34). Thus it is evident that great harm was being wrought by the Corinthians' coming together at the Lord's table; the abuses were temporally and spiritually detrimental to them. Participating in the Lord's Supper unworthily is equal to sinning against the body and blood of Christ. Those who drink unworthily bring judgment upon themselves. One must search their heart and mind before participating in the solemn act of the Lord's Supper. Paul's advice to discern the Lord's body and blood may mean two things. It may first mean recognizing the objective reality, that Christ's body and blood are truly present. This should create a sense of reverence instead of a party spirit when the church comes together for worship. Second, Christians must equally recognize what the Lord's Supper is intended to nurture and represent: the oneness of believers in unity (1 Cor 10:17). If the Corinthians would take time to judge their actions and intentions before partaking of the bread and wine, a divine judgment would not fall upon them. Those who participate in the celebration of the Lord's Supper must see beyond the physical nature of the bread and wine to what they represent—the broken body and the shed blood of Christ for the justification and reconciliation of sinners.

QUESTIONS FOR PERSONAL REFLECTION

1. What does the metaphor of the "head" mean? Why did Paul use this metaphor?
2. Why is the Lord's Supper so significant, and why is it so important that it must be done right?
3. What were the underlying causes of the behavioral aberration that was manifested by the Corinthians during the Lord's Supper?
4. What should be the focus of the Lord's Supper? Personal introspection and confession, or the unity and loving fellowship of the community?
5. What are the possible consequences of participating in the Lord's Supper without having the right attitudes?

1 Corinthians 12:1–31

One Body, Many Members

THE CHAPTER BEGINS PAUL'S long discussion about spiritual gifts (chapters 12–14), a subject of utmost importance both to the Corinthians, to whom Paul originally wrote, and to believers today. God has given believers certain gifts for serving him. These are Spirit-bestowed gifts, and they will vary with the Christian. Each one is fully responsible to use all that God has graciously bestowed him or her with. There are two extremes to avoid. On the one hand, one must not overestimate human abilities and underrate the gifts of the Spirit, acting as if they were not only unnecessary but also extinct. On the other hand, one must avoid the arrogance that results from a person's consideration of his or her giftedness as being superior to that of others.

CONCERNING SPIRITUAL GIFTS (12:1–3)

> 1 Now concerning spiritual *gifts*, brethren, I do not want you to be unaware.
> 2 You know that when you were pagans, *you were* led astray to the mute idols, however you were led.
> 3 Therefore I make known to you that no one speaking by the Spirit of God says, "Jesus is accursed"; and no one can say, "Jesus is Lord," except by the Holy Spirit.

The introduction demonstrates the importance that Paul attached to the topic. He does not want the Corinthians to be ignorant or uninformed. This is one of three important truths of which Paul, in his letters, specifically would not want his readers to be ignorant. They were not to be ignorant of

God's plan for Israel (Rom 11:25), of spiritual gifts (1 Cor 12:1), and about the second coming of Jesus (1 Thess 4:13). Sadly, so many Christians are ignorant on these exact points! Although the literal translation of verse 1 suggests "spiritual things or spiritual persons," the addition of gifts is appropriate here, given the context. Because of their idolatrous background, the Corinthians were not prone to a misunderstanding of the gifts.

Many times, past teaching and experiences contribute to a poor understanding of the Holy Spirit and the gifts. In a congregation such as Corinth's, where supernatural manifestations are taking place, it is important to make a distinction between those gifts that find their source in God as well as those which do not. At the start, Paul lays down a broad principle for discerning matters regarding spiritual gifts: *judge things by how they relate to Jesus Christ*. "Therefore I make known to you that no one speaking by the Spirit of God calls Jesus accursed" (v. 3a). One must ask important questions such as "Does a supposed spiritual gift glorify Jesus or is it for self–promotion?" "Does it promote the true Jesus or a false one?"

SAME SPIRIT, SAME LORD, SAME GOD WHO GIVES THE GIFTS (12:4–6)

> 4 Now there are varieties of gifts, but the same Spirit.
>
> 5 And there are varieties of ministries, and the same Lord.
>
> 6 There are varieties of effects, but the same God who works all things in all *persons*.

Paul's description of the gifts begins both with their nature and source. Paul uses three important words: "gifts" (v. 4, Greek *charismata*); "administration "(KJV), or literally "services" (v. 5, Greek *diakonia*), and "operations" (KJV), or literally "workings" (v. 6, Greek *energemata*). His choice of words is not merely stylistic. While the gifts (*charismata*) emphasize the truth of the spiritual manifestations as an expression of God's grace, the administration or services (*diakonia*) suggest that the purpose of the gifts is not for self-enjoyment or edification. Rather the gifts are for loving ministry within the body of Christ. The operations or workings (*energemata*) suggests that in all these manifestations, God is powerfully at work through the Spirit. However, although these "diversities" go under different names, they are interchangeable labels.

Although it is hard to say whether Paul has a trinitarian concept, he nevertheless expresses the source of the gifts in strongly trinitarian terms

ONE BODY, MANY MEMBERS

(vv. 4–6). The source of the gifts is the Triune God—the Spirit, the Lord, and God. It is not the Spirit alone who distributes the gifts. Paul accentuates the coherence of the gifts that God distributes as a unity-in-diversity, thus leaving no room for rivalry and competition within the body of Christ. Paul will develop this theme later in verses 12–30. One particular gift must not and cannot be viewed as superior to the others; all come from the same God. His emphasis on unity-in-diversity in verses 4–6 is rooted in the nature of the one, holy and triune God.

DIFFERING GIFTS ARE GIVEN FOR THE COMMON GOOD (12:7–11)

> 7 But to each one is given the manifestation of the Spirit for the common good.
> 8 For to one is given the word of wisdom through the Spirit, and to another the word of knowledge according to the same Spirit;
> 9 to another faith by the same Spirit, and to another gifts of healing by the one Spirit,
> 10 and to another the effecting of miracles, and to another prophecy, and to another the distinguishing of spirits, to another *various* kinds of tongues, and to another the interpretation of tongues.
> 11 But one and the same Spirit works all these things, distributing to each one individually just as He wills.

In verse 7, Paul indicates that the gifts are given to all the people of God for the benefit of all or the common good. God gives these gifts for the edification of the body. The gifts are not to bring personal benefit, advantage, or status to the individual, but to give an advantage to the whole community. This advantage consists of building up the body of Christ into his image. After speaking in general terms, Paul mentions different manifestations of the Spirit in verses 8–10. He begins by mentioning the word of wisdom. This is the unique ability to speak forth the wisdom of God, especially in an important situation, as shown in Solomon (1 Kgs 3:16–18), Jesus (Luke 20:20–26), Stephen (Acts 7), and Paul (Acts 23). This is followed by the word of knowledge. This gift has been the subject of different interpretations. A Pentecostal preacher once defined it as "a divinely granted flash of revelation concerning things which were hopelessly hidden from the senses," citing the example of God's judgment for Eli, given as a voice in the night to Samuel (1 Sam 3:13) and God's word to Peter regarding the arrival of messengers from Cornelius (Acts 10:19). Next on the list is the gift of faith. Without a doubt, Paul is not referring to the initial faith that is necessary for salvation. Though faith is an essential part of every Christian's life, the gift of faith is the unique ability to trust God against all circumstances, as Peter did when he walked out of the boat on onto the water (Matt 14:22–33). Next are the "gifts of healing." It is important to note that the word gift is an indefinite plural, which may suggest that the gifts are bestowed upon some believers commensurate with the illnesses present. Moreover, it is to be observed that these gifts are for the benefit of the community. This is followed by "working of miracles," which seems to be a general term, encompassing supernatural activity, including healing. In most cases, the Holy Spirit overrides the power of nature. The gift of prophecy refers both to the foretelling of the future as well as the forthtelling of the mind of God for a particular situation. Those who believe that the miraculous gifts have ceased wish to define prophecy as "preaching." Though this is common, it is inaccurate. There are different words for preaching, and for divinely inspired speech. Paul is using the word for divinely inspired speech, not preaching. It is totally inaccurate to define prophecy as good preaching. "Distinguishing between spirits" or "discerning of spirits" (KJV) describes the God-given ability to determine whether a supernatural manifestation has its source in God or not. An example is that of Paul in Acts (16:16–18). The list continues with "speaking in different kinds of tongues." This refers to a supernatural utterance in a language that was not learned by the speaker, and it may or may not be a language known to others. Lastly, Paul mentions the "interpretation of tongues." Essentially, this refers to an intelligible presentation of the content of what was spoken in an unknown tongue. Having listed the gifts, again, in verse 11, Paul reiterates the one source of the gifts—the Spirit. He goes on to proffer another reason for unity, and a reason against any sense of superiority regarding the gifts. They are distributed not according to human will, but as the Spirit of God wills.

ONE SPIRIT, ONE BODY (12:12–13)

> 12 For even as the body is one and *yet* has many members, and all the members of the body, though they are many, are one body, so also is Christ.

> 13 For by one Spirit we were all baptized into one body, whether Jews or Greeks, whether slaves or free, and we were all made to drink of one Spirit.

Paul is now about to explain further what he summarily stated in verse 7, that the gifts are given for the advantage of all. Paul was concerned that the Corinthians' distorted view of the gifts has led to a lack of social cohesion among them. To correct the problem, Paul insists that the Corinthians have all been immersed (baptized) in one Spirit into the body of Christ. So Paul employs the analogy of the human body to drive home the points that he has been making in verses 4–11.

ONE BODY, MANY MEMBERS (12:14–20)

> 14 For the body is not one member, but many.
> 15 If the foot says, "Because I am not a hand, I am not *a part* of the body," it is not for this reason any the less *a part* of the body.
> 16 And if the ear says, "Because I am not an eye, I am not *a part* of the body," it is not for this reason any the less *a part* of the body.
> 17 If the whole body were an eye, where would the hearing be? If the whole were hearing, where would the sense of smell be?
> 18 But now God has placed the members, each one of them, in the body, just as He desired.
> 19 If they were all one member, where would the body be?
> 20 But now there are many members, but one body.

How are we to think of the gathering together of believers? Paul introduces the metaphor of the human body, something which must have been readily understood by the Corinthians. Just as it is totally absurd to think that the body is made up of only the most noticeable parts, so it is to think that the body could function without its less prominent parts. As such, there is no room for either an inferiority or superiority complex within the body. Each part of the body needs the other in order to function well. So is the body of Christ. We need each other to function as God intends. By application, no one of the gifts is by itself sufficient.

1 CORINTHIANS

MANY MEMBERS, ONE PURPOSE (12:21–27)

> 21 And the eye cannot say to the hand, "I have no need of you"; or again the head to the feet, "I have no need of you."
>
> 22 On the contrary, it is much truer that the members of the body which seem to be weaker are necessary;
>
> 23 and those *members* of the body which we deem less honorable, on these we bestow more abundant honor, and our less presentable members become much more presentable,
>
> 24 whereas our more presentable members have no need *of it*. But God has *so* composed the body, giving more abundant honor to that *member* which lacked,
>
> 25 so that there may be no division in the body, but *that* the members may have the same care for one another.
>
> 26 And if one member suffers, all the members suffer with it; if *one* member is honored, all the members rejoice with it.
>
> 27 Now you are Christ's body, and individually members of it.

Paul uses the body metaphor to argue that no believer be seen as less important than the other. In the body every part is important. As the saying goes, "The ground is level at the foot of the cross." The main message of verses 21–27 is quite clear. Some parts of the body that we regard as lacking honor are absolutely essential for our survival. Those parts play an even more indispensable role in sustaining the life of the body than, say, the eye or ear. The body parts that we cover for the sake of modesty are not disgusting; we cannot survive without them. The application to Corinth and to the church today is unmistakably clear. Those who may appear to flaunt more spectacular gifts may actually turn out to be less indispensable than the quiet, faithful, prayerful, devoted, humble members whose values and contributions are often overlooked by those who seek power. Paul's overriding concern is with the unity of the social body of the church, which he expresses in terms of a concern for the wholeness of the physical body: "That there be no discord in the body, but that the members may have the same care for one another" (12:25). Thus, a sense of group identity supersedes a sense of individualism; bodily wholeness is thus maintained.

GOD'S GIFTS (12:28–31)

> 28 And God has appointed in the church, first apostles, second prophets, third teachers, then miracles, then gifts of healings, helps, administrations, *various* kinds of tongues.

> 29 All are not apostles, are they? All are not prophets, are they? All are not teachers, are they? All are not *workers of* miracles, are they?
> 30 All do not have gifts of healings, do they? All do not speak with tongues, do they? All do not interpret, do they?
> 31 But earnestly desire the greater gifts.
> And I show you a still more excellent way.

Paul ends chapter 12 with a list of some of the gifts that God gives to various individuals. There are three important observations. First, it is to be noted that the list does not exactly match the list that Paul provided earlier in 12:8–10, something that must alert us to the lack of comprehensiveness of the former. Paul discusses the ministry functions in dialog with the existing situation at Corinth, as well as in the light of the forms of leadership that suited his own cultural context. Paul does not suggest that these offices are either the only or exact forms of leadership that are both timeless or universally normative.

Second, in context, these verses press home Paul's argument in the entire chapter by way of summary. If these gifts are given generously as God wills (vv. 4–6), and if they are for the common good of the whole church (v. 4), it is right to say that the gifts cannot and must not serve the purpose of comparison and competition among ministers for the sake of enhancing one's status. The members of Christ's body ought not to be in competition with one another to gain prestige, position, or power. Rather, they should work together for the well-being of the whole assembly. Moreover, it is significant to note that Paul does not suggest that there is any particular individual who functions in all these capacities. The gifts transcend the capacity of any individual to possess them. Significantly, these gifts are complementary. They function together within the community—the church. As such, the passage poses a challenge to any self-styled leader who assumes that he or she is the "answer" or "solution" without reference to the gifts of others. Also, the attitude of selecting certain leaders as "models" of chosen spiritual attributes flies in the face of Paul's discussion here.

Third, the gifts are God-given. In the same manner that the church does not bestow the gifts of healings, tongues, and interpretation of tongues, etc., upon individuals, the church does not create apostles, prophets, teachers, or other ministry gifts. They are Spirit-given.

In verse 28, Paul lists five gifts, starting with that of the apostle. This has raised two questions, the first of which is whether Paul intended to

1 CORINTHIANS

grade the gifts, thereby creating a hierarchical structure, or he is simply enumerating the gifts. Without a doubt, Paul did not intend to create a hierarchical structure. However, the list suggests some priority being given to apostles, prophets, and teachers. The second question relates to whether Paul intentionally moves from "gifts" (*charismata*) to roles or offices in the church. Probably so. The climax of Paul's argument comes in verses 29–30. He does not think that everyone will have every gift or fill every role in the body of Christ. The diversity of the gifts within the body of Christ is not only acceptable or expected, it is God's plan for how the body of Christ would function. Thus, Paul's argument comes in a full circle. Verse 31 is a transitional statement that not only looks back to the discussion in 12:1–30, but also anticipates the discussion that is to follow in chapter 13. Paul told the Corinthians to eagerly desire the greater gifts.

QUESTIONS FOR PERSONAL REFLECTION

1. What is the source of the "spiritual gifts" and what is their purpose?
2. What are the results of the proper use of spiritual gifts?
3. Why are "diversity" and "unity" both necessary within a congregation?
4. How significant is Paul's use of the "body" metaphor? What part of the body, if any, is dispensable? What are the implications for the individual and the community?
5. How can I be certain that I have spiritual gifts?

1 Corinthians 13:1–13

Love: The More Excellent Way

1 CORINTHIANS 13 IS one of the most familiar chapters in the New Testament. It is no coincidence that it is located at this particular point in the argument of the letter. It focuses on love, a subject that is found throughout Paul's discussion of worship, and emphasizes the importance of the upbuilding of others. The chapter not only provides an answer to the Corinthians' attitude to the exercise of spiritual gifts, but also proffers a solution to the divisiveness that was at the root of almost all their problems. Paul shows them a more excellent way—a way that stands in sharp contrast to theirs.

THE PREEMINENCE OF LOVE (13:1–3)

> 1 If I speak with the tongues of men and of angels, but do not have love, I have become a noisy gong or a clanging cymbal.
>
> 2 If I have *the gift of* prophecy, and know all mysteries and all knowledge; and if I have all faith, so as to remove mountains, but do not have love, I am nothing.
>
> 3 And if I give all my possessions to feed *the poor*, and if I surrender my body to be burned, but do not have love, it profits me nothing.

The Corinthians were fascinated with spiritual gifts, particularly the gift of tongues, but Paul reminds them even the gift of tongues is meaningless without love. Without love, a person may speak with the gift of tongues, but it is as meaningless as sounding brass or a tinkling cymbal. It is nothing but empty noise. The Greek word translated as "tongues" (*glossais*) has the simple idea of "languages" in some places (Acts 2:11; Rev 5:9). Hence, some conclude that the gift of tongues is simply the ability to communicate the gospel in other languages—it is the capability of learning languages quickly. However, its usage here shows that it also usually does refer to a supernatural language by which a believer communicates with God. There is no other way the reference to tongues of angels can be understood in this context.

Paul goes on to say that prophecy, knowledge, and faith to do miracles are likewise irrelevant apart from love. Giving oneself to be burnt is a barren gesture unless it is inspired by love. Paul's point is unmistakably clear: the Corinthian Christians were majoring in the minor; they were missing the motive and the goal of the gifts, making the means to become their own end. So, Paul draws their attention back to the preeminence of love. Love trumps all. As said earlier, one must understand that, for Paul, it is not an issue of love versus the gifts. Neither must it be for us either. For that matter, a person or a church should never be forced to choose between love and gifts of the Holy Spirit. Paul is stressing the focus and end of the gifts: love, not the gifts for their own sake. Each of the spiritual gifts is great and, together, they constitute a formidable power. But their motivation and purpose are ineffectual unless they are guided by love.

WHAT LOVE IS (13:4–7)

> 4 Love is patient, love is kind *and* is not jealous; love does not brag *and* is not arrogant,
>
> 5 does not act unbecomingly; it does not seek its own, is not provoked, does not take into account a wrong *suffered*,
>
> 6 does not rejoice in unrighteousness, but rejoices with the truth;
>
> 7 bears all things, believes all things, hopes all things, endures all things.

Although it has often been taken as a description of Christ's character, and rightly so, in verses 4–7 Paul shows how a Christian ought to behave and how, he, as the apostle to the Corinthians, has been attempting to behave. Love is a matter of behavior, an other-directed behavior for that matter, and not feeling. Such is the character of Christian love. The word *agape*, which is likely derived from the Septuagint (the Greek translation of the Old Testament), is often used of God's love, not ordinary human love. What a great privilege it is, then, for the Christian to be a bearer, by means of God's Spirit, of God's love.

It is important to note from the onset of the description of the characteristics of love that it is not an abstract, airy concept. It is described with action words. Paul is not writing about how he feels or how he expects the Corinthians to feel. Rather, it is about what they should be as Christians. True love is always demonstrated by action. Love suffers long. It is the type of love that characterizes One of whom the Scripture says that "the Lord is not slack concerning His promise, as some count slackness, but is longsuffering toward us, not willing that any should perish but that all should come to repentance" (2 Pet 3:9). If God's love is in us, we will be longsuffering to those who annoy us and hurt us. Love is kind. Kindness is demonstrated in simple acts such as giving a cup of cold water to the thirsty (Matt 25:42).

In verses 4b–6, Paul enumerates eight things love does not do. First, love does not envy. Whereas jealousy says that "I would like to have what you have," envy says, "I wish you do not have what you have." Envy is one of the least productive and most damaging of all sins to those who allow it. It accomplishes nothing, except to hurt the one who harbors it. But love keeps its distance from envy and does not resent it when someone else is promoted or blessed. Love does not parade itself: Love in action can work anonymously. It does not have to have the limelight or the attention to do a good job, or to be satisfied with the result. Love gives because it loves to give, not out of the sense of praise it can have from showing itself off.

Love is not puffed up: To be puffed up is to be arrogant and self-focused. Love does not allow its head to swell, but focuses on the needs of others. Love does not behave rudely—that is, it is not ill-mannered or brash. Where there is love, there will be kindness and good manners. A person who loves does not just speak his or her mind, but minds his or her speech. Love does not seek its own (an idea that Paul expresses in a slightly different manner in Romans 12:10 and Philippians 2:4). This is being like Jesus in a most basic way, being an others-centered person instead of a self-centered person. Love is not easily provoked. This is perhaps the aspect of love that is the most difficult to understand. In plain language, love is neither touchy nor irritable. Love thinks no evil. It does not store up the memory or keep an account of any wrong it has received. It puts away the hurts of the past instead of clinging to them. After all, nobody is more hurt by bitterness than the person who keeps it. Love does not rejoice in iniquity. "I told you so" and "It serves you right" are familiar statements, but they are not the language of love. Love desires the best for others and does not derive personal satisfaction from the failure of others. Instead, love rejoices in the truth.

Paul ends the discussion of the characteristics of love on a positive note. He states that love bears all things, believes all things, hopes all things, and endures all things. The word *panta*, translated "all," can also be translated as "always." Paul's point is that love never tires of support, never loses faith, and never gives up hope. Most of us can bear all things, and believe all things, and hope all things, but only for a while! The greatness of agape love is that it keeps on bearing, believing, and hoping. It does not give up.

AN EVERLASTING LOVE (13:8)

> 8 Love never fails; but if *there are gifts of* prophecy, they will be done away; if *there are* tongues, they will cease; if *there is* knowledge, it will be done away.

The verse begins the concluding paragraph of the chapter. Here Paul attests to the permanence of love as he continues to put the spiritual gifts and virtues in perspective. Love never fails. Paul is addressing the over-emphasis the Corinthian Christians had on the other gifts of the Holy Spirit. He shows that they should emphasize love more than the gifts because the gifts are temporary "containers" of God's work; love is the work itself. The spiritual gifts remain for the present, but are imperfect and will eventually come to an end. However, there is no warrant in the verse to conclude that the miraculous gifts ended with the apostles. Paul does not give the slightest hint of such interpretation. Obviously, knowledge did not pass away with Paul. Neither can it be justified to say that the church today has entered its time of perfection. The fact that one does not appreciate tongues and prophecy as legitimate gifts neither invalidates them nor justifies their being wished away.

ENDURING LOVE (13:9–13)

> 9 For we know in part and we prophesy in part;
>> 10 but when the perfect comes, the partial will be done away.
>> 11 When I was a child, I used to speak like a child, think like a child, reason like a child; when I became a man, I did away with childish things.

Love: The More Excellent Way

> 12 For now we see in a mirror dimly, but then face to face; now I know in part, but then I will know fully just as I also have been fully known.
>
> 13 But now faith, hope, love, abide these three; but the greatest of these is love.

Paul gives the reason why other gifts apart from love will cease. Those gifts, such as prophecy or knowledge, are specifically meant to equip the believer to endure in this age. The milieu in which they operate will one day come to an end and will be superseded by a situation in which they become unnecessary or inappropriate. Paul likens the situation to that of growing up. There is a life appropriate to a child. Such is manifested in thought, speech, and reasoning power. But when adulthood arrives, these characteristics are no longer viable and, as such, must be left behind. Tongues will cease when the Lord returns and completes his plan for Christians. Partial knowledge such as the Corinthians and Christians now have will be brought to completion. Not so love. Therefore, all gifts (except love) can be characterized as partial.

In mistaking the part for the whole and the partial for the final, the Corinthians, unlike Paul, are childish. It is wrong to suggest that verses 11–12 view speaking in tongues and prophecy as childishness, particularly because Paul himself claims to do both. What Paul is saying is that there is an age appropriate to do so, and now is that age. When the completion of that age finally arrives, then it will be time to set aside what was appropriate and needful for that age. For Paul, the three great pursuits of the Christian life are not miracles, power, and gifts, but faith, hope, and love. Though the gifts are precious and given by the Holy Spirit today, they were never meant to be the focus or goal of our Christian lives. Instead, we must pursue faith, hope, and love.

In conclusion, it is appropriate to say that Paul's discussion in this chapter is not only powerful, but also heart-searching. It calls for a careful examination of our motivation for service. There is a reason why Paul put this chapter in the midst of his discussion of spiritual gifts. Paul wants the Corinthian Christians to remember that giftedness is not the measure of maturity; the display of love is. Each Christian must ask themselves: Am I exercising God's gift out of love, in order to glorify him and bless others, or do I have a secret motive or desire to enhance myself, to receive human praise, to cover up some deep personal problem, or to appear more spiritual than others? We must allow the Holy Spirit to purify our motives. We must do all things, and respond to all situations, out of love. We must desire to love. Love is a choice! Paul's discussion of love is not meant to persuade the Corinthians to abandon their prized spiritual gifts. Rather, it is intended to convince them to exercise their gifts with love. If otherwise exercised, they are spiritually unfruitful or barren.

QUESTIONS FOR PERSONAL REFLECTION

1. What is the relationship between "love" and the "gifts"? Can one function with the other? If so, what are the consequences?
2. What would be your reaction to someone who, having read this chapter, would still conclude that there are people that he or she could not love?
3. Why do you think Paul says that love is greater than faith and hope?
4. In what ways can I show love to a fellow believer?

1 Corinthians 14:1–40

Spiritual Gifts and Edification

PAUL HAS SPOKEN IN the previous chapter regarding love as the context in which the spiritual gifts should operate. He now resumes his teachings concerning the gifts that began in chapter 12, focusing on the issue of intelligibility and order during the worship service. The somewhat disorderly situation in Corinth required that Paul pay more attention to the gifts of speaking in tongues and prophecy. Perhaps some Corinthians were misusing speaking in tongues, resulting in others in the congregation being against its use and wanting it stopped. For Paul, whatever is done in the church should be for God's glory, the edification of other believers, and the sake of a witness to the unsaved. We must not gather simply to entertain one another.

AN URGENT EXHORTATION: PURSUE LOVE (14:1)

> 1 Pursue love, yet desire earnestly spiritual *gifts*, but especially that you may prophesy.

Paul begins the section by affirming the superiority of prophecy to tongues. The reason prophecy is superior to tongues is that it is understandable. After having stressed the preeminence of love, Paul wants those in the church to excel at edifying others with their spiritual gifts, as an application of that love. Prophecy is to be preferred to uninterpreted tongues because, in the case of tongues, no one is edified unless the tongues are interpreted (vv. 1–6). In verse 1, Paul is telling the Corinthians to make love the object of their pursuit. It speaks of intensity, perseverance, and an attitude that always achieves its goal. The present imperative form indicates a continuous and ongoing pursuit of love. Paul understood that there is much to distract a person in the Christian life. Unless one determines to pursue love constantly and intensely as the motivating and guiding principle of life, some other lesser motivation will emerge and begin to direct one's life. This obviously provides a conclusion to chapter 13. Paul's second command in verse 1 is for the Corinthians to strive for, or desire, the spiritual gifts. The verb "desire" is the same word used in 1 Corinthians 12:31.

PROPHECY VERSUS TONGUES IN THE EDIFICATION OF THE CHURCH (14:2–6)

> 2 For one who speaks in a tongue does not speak to men but to God; for no one understands, but in *his* spirit he speaks mysteries.
>
> 3 But one who prophesies speaks to men for edification and exhortation and consolation.
>
> 4 One who speaks in a tongue edifies himself; but one who prophesies edifies the church.
>
> 5 Now I wish that you all spoke in tongues, but *even* more that you would prophesy; and greater is one who prophesies than one who speaks in tongues, unless he interprets, so that the church may receive edifying.
>
> 6 But now, brethren, if I come to you speaking in tongues, what will I profit you unless I speak to you either by way of revelation or of knowledge or of prophecy or of teaching?

The reason Paul commands the Corinthians to pursue love and seek to prophesy is given in verses 2–4. Paul clearly shows the contrast between prophecy and tongues in verses 2–4. People who speak in a tongue do so in communication with God. The two main issues here are intelligibility and the upbuilding or edification of the whole assembly. A person that speaks in tongues can speak mysteries in the Spirit, but such speech has no beneficial result in the congregation if it cannot be understood.

Verse 3 identifies content for prophecy. In prophecy, the speaker speaks edification, exhortation (encouragement), and comfort to other people. Paul first used the word "edification" in its verb form in 1 Corinthians 8:1 when he wrote "Love builds up." The same verb appears in 1 Corinthians 8:10; 10:23; twice in 14:4; and in 14:17. Thus "edification" is one of the pivotal concepts for Paul in his problems with the church at Corinth. Without doubt, "edification" is a criterion that Paul uses to evaluate the appropriateness of behavior. If an action builds up the church, it is beneficial. It is clear from his writings that Paul thought of edification primarily in terms of the local Christian community. His ministry was to "build up and not to destroy" (2 Cor 10:8; 13:10). It is clear that, for Paul, edification does not primarily refer to individuals whose goal is to mature to spiritual, individual personalities, but rather to the church, which, for Paul, exists in local concrete communities.

Paul directly states the issue in verse 4. Those who speak in a tongue edify or build up themselves. Those who prophesy edify or build up the church. It is the building up of the church that matters, not the building up of oneself. Verse 5 attempts to soften the impact of this contrast. Paul states that he wishes that all the Corinthians spoke in tongues. However, he would rather they all prophesied. Prophesying is greater than speaking in tongues unless someone interprets the tongue. Interpretation allows the possibility for a "message from God' to be conveyed to the congregation by the utterance spoken in tongues. That offers the opportunity for the "obedience" (hearing) mentioned in verse 2. Verse 5 concludes with Paul's main point again: edification. Interpretation allows the congregation to be built up or edified.

SOUNDS AND SIGNIFICATION (14:7–12)

> 7 Yet *even* lifeless things, either flute or harp, in producing a sound, if they do not produce a distinction in the tones, how will it be known what is played on the flute or on the harp?
>
> 8 For if the bugle produces an indistinct sound, who will prepare himself for battle?
>
> 9 So also you, unless you utter by the tongue speech that is clear, how will it be known what is spoken? For you will be speaking into the air.
>
> 10 There are, perhaps, a great many kinds of languages in the world, and no *kind* is without meaning.
>
> 11 If then I do not know the meaning of the language, I will be to the one who speaks a barbarian, and the one who speaks will be a barbarian to me.
>
> 12 So also you, since you are zealous of spiritual *gifts*, seek to abound for the edification of the church.

Paul now reinforces his point by the use of three analogies. In verses 7–11, Paul illustrates what he means by uninterpreted tongues through the use of musical instruments and languages unknown to a speaker. Paul's main point is that, whatever the type of sound, mere sound produces no real effect on the hearer unless it exhibits some order, pattern, or meaning. In his first analogy, Paul cites flutes and harps. If the players of these instruments make no clear distinction in their tones, no recognizable tune will be produced. Musical instruments must use a certain pitch and beat to communicate a song. If they do not, the music is not accessible to the listener. Sounds are coming forth, but they cannot be understood. The trumpet that makes an uncertain sound is of no profit for others. An indistinct trumpet call will rouse no soldier to battle. As an example, there is what is known as the "talking drum" in Southwest Nigeria. It is used both for celebration and declaration of hostilities. Paul's third analogy is drawn from languages. There are many different languages in the world, but unless one understands the force, the intent, of what is being said by a foreign speaker, his words will be mere gibberish to the hearer.

Paul draws the argument to a conclusion in verse 12. Once again, he affirms his central argument that the Corinthians ought to seek to use their gifts for the edification of the church. Speaking in tongues, without conveying an intelligible message does not build up the Christian community. Since the Corinthians are eager for gifts of the Spirit, let them aspire above all to excel in those which build up the church.

THE MIND AND THE SPIRIT (14:13–19)

13 Therefore let one who speaks in a tongue pray that he may interpret.

14 For if I pray in a tongue, my spirit prays, but my mind is unfruitful.

15 What is *the outcome* then? I will pray with the spirit and I will pray with the mind also; I will sing with the spirit and I will sing with the mind also.

16 Otherwise if you bless in the spirit *only*, how will the one who fills the place of the ungifted say the "Amen" at your giving of thanks, since he does not know what you are saying?

17 For you are giving thanks well enough, but the other person is not edified.

18 I thank God, I speak in tongues more than you all;

19 however, in the church I desire to speak five words with my mind so that I may instruct others also, rather than ten thousand words in a tongue.

In verses 13–19, he stresses the need for the interpretation of tongues in prayer and worship so that the believer who does not have the gift of interpretation (which would be the majority of them) may benefit. Having made the point, at some length, that speaking in tongues without interpretation fails to edify, Paul now urges anyone who speaks in tongues to pray for the further gift of being able to interpret what they say (v. 13). Paul then reverts again to the theme of the inadequacy of uninterpreted tongue-speaking. As previously, he stresses its ineffectiveness for edification, but first he makes the point that it is of limited value for the speaker himself (v. 14). This is because it is an activity in which a person's rational mind is not fully engaged. The expression "my mind" is sometimes used by Paul in an inclusive sense to refer to my whole being, being thus equivalent to "me" (see e.g. 2 Cor 2:13; cf. Gal 6:18). More fundamentally, however, it refers to "me" as capable of a relationship with God (see, e.g., Rom 1:9; 8:16).

So Paul is saying two things here about praying in tongues: it is the expression of a real relationship with God, yet it does not engage my reason. In verse 15, Paul mentions two distinct activities: on the one hand, praying and praising in tongues and, on the other, praying and praising in intelligible words. He intends to continue doing both. He then reverts in the next verses to his previous point that tongue-speaking, when not accompanied by interpretation, does nothing for the bystander. Lest his remarks be misconstrued as a denigration or total rejection of tongues, Paul gives thanks to God that he is more gifted in tongues than any of his readers (v. 18).

REORDER YOUR THINKING (14:20–25)

> 20 Brethren, do not be children in your thinking; yet in evil be infants, but in your thinking be mature.
>
> 21 In the Law it is written, "By men of strange tongues and by the lips of strangers I will speak to this people, and even so they will not listen to Me," says the Lord.
>
> 22 So then tongues are for a sign, not to those who believe but to unbelievers; but prophecy *is for a sign*, not to unbelievers but to those who believe.
>
> 23 Therefore if the whole church assembles together and all speak in tongues, and ungifted men or unbelievers enter, will they not say that you are mad?
>
> 24 But if all prophesy, and an unbeliever or an ungifted man enters, he is convicted by all, he is called to account by all;

1 CORINTHIANS

> 25 the secrets of his heart are disclosed; and so he will fall on his face and worship God, declaring that God is certainly among you.

Paul's statements in these verses constitute a practical application of the issue of intelligibility in worship, an issue that is connected with edification. The Corinthians need to reorder their thinking concerning their disproportionate emphasis on tongues. The childishness and lack of maturity (conveyed by Paul's use of *nepion*) of the Corinthians are both evidenced by their exaltation of the gift of tongues. These words would probably have raised the eyebrows of his readers, who clearly prided themselves on their maturity (2:6). Basically, what Paul does here is invite his readers to consider the effect upon uninstructed persons, or unbelievers, first of entering a service of worship where everyone is speaking in tongues, and secondly a gathering where all are prophesying. In the former, a visitor could easily have reached the conclusion that the worshipers were all mad. In the latter, however, the visitor would hear something that searched his or her conscience and brought conviction, revealing the secrets of his or her heart, and thus be forced to worship and acknowledge that God was indeed in their midst.

ORDER IN PUBLIC WORSHIP (14:25–40)

> 26 What is *the outcome* then, brethren? When you assemble, each one has a psalm, has a teaching, has a revelation, has a tongue, has an interpretation. Let all things be done for edification.
> 27 If anyone speaks in a tongue, *it should be* by two or at the most three, and *each* in turn, and one must interpret;
> 28 but if there is no interpreter, he must keep silent in the church; and let him speak to himself and to God.
> 29 Let two or three prophets speak, and let the others pass judgment.
> 30 But if a revelation is made to another who is seated, the first one must keep silent.
> 31 For you can all prophesy one by one, so that all may learn and all may be exhorted;
> 32 and the spirits of prophets are subject to prophets;
> 33 for God is not *a God* of confusion but of peace, as in all the churches of the saints.

> 34 The women are to keep silent in the churches; for they are not permitted to speak, but are to subject themselves, just as the Law also says.
>
> 35 If they desire to learn anything, let them ask their own husbands at home; for it is improper for a woman to speak in church.
>
> 36 Was it from you that the word of God *first* went forth? Or has it come to you only?
>
> 37 If anyone thinks he is a prophet or spiritual, let him recognize that the things which I write to you are the Lord's commandment.
>
> 38 But if anyone does not recognize *this*, he is not recognized.
>
> 39 Therefore, my brethren, desire earnestly to prophesy, and do not forbid to speak in tongues.
>
> 40 But all things must be done properly and in an orderly manner.

Paul's argument for the superior value of prophecy over tongues in gatherings of the community for worship has come in a full circle. Now he proceeds to apply the principles he has been expounding to the Corinthian situation and set guidelines for the use of tongues and prophecy in worship. The Corinthian Church must have been unstructured and participatory in worship (v. 26). It was a "charismatic" styled church rather than one with ordered worship or sermon time. Paul is not suggesting that all the aspects of worship listed in verse 26 should take place at any particular given worship service, but that whatever the Corinthians did in worship, it should upbuild the body. Whatever their individual gifts, all are to aim to edify the church (cf. 14:3–5, 12, 17, 26). Paul then moves to restore some order and gives precise instructions to regulate speaking in tongues. Paul does not prohibit the use of tongues in worship. Rather, he sought to limit it and give it order (v. 27). As in verse 2, Paul acknowledges that speaking in tongues is a true means of communication with God. But no spiritual self-indulgence is to be allowed in church. So, without interpretation, a tongue-speaker must keep silent (v. 28). In verses 29–31, Paul gives similar instructions for the regulation of prophecy. Prophetic utterances are to be weighed. They are not to be accepted uncritically, without questioning and discussion. As such, no single prophet has the absolute say. Moreover, Paul says that the spirits of prophets are subject to the prophets (v. 32). Paul then addresses the issue of wives speaking in the church. The particular problem that Paul addresses remains a matter of conjecture. However, while the verses remain controversial, one thing remains clear. The key for Paul is that worship be orderly in order that God may be glorified by everything that takes place, and unbelievers will find Christianity attractive rather than repulsive (v. 33–35). This should be our goal today, and it is the responsibility of both male and female congregants. All other debates are counterproductive. Paul assumes that women can prophesy in 1 Corinthians 11:2–16, and 1 Corinthians 14:34–35 cannot and must not be used to prevent women from speaking of a spiritual nature. God values both men and women equally and speaks through both.

Paul now concludes the chapter with a sharp rebuke and an assertion of his own authority, before summing up the thrust of the chapter in two pithy sentences. The Corinthian Christians, like many present-day denominations, acted as if they were the only Christians in the universe. Paul let them see that they were a part of something much bigger, and as such needed to submit themselves to God's will for the church as a whole (v. 36). Hence, Paul saw the importance for charismatic prophecies to be tested and tried. He then moves on to claim the right to speak for God and assert his authority over any prophet who might claim not to be subject to his rules (v. 37). Not all who think of themselves as spiritual are truly spiritual. Anyone who supposes that he or she is a prophet or spiritual person should recognize Paul's authority (v. 38).

Verses 39–40 conclude Paul's argument in the chapter. One must note that Paul gently steers the Corinthians away from tongues in public worship toward prophecy. He does not forbid tongues, for he accepts it as a legitimate gift from God. Paul does not intend to "quench or put out the Spirit's fire" (1 Thess 5:19). He restates the underlying principle behind his entire admonition in the chapter: "But all things should be done decently and in order" (v. 40). The concepts of order and peace manifest themselves differently in different cultures, as well as in different denominations and groups. Therefore we must refrain from judging too quickly or condemning those whom we perceive are not doing things exactly the same way that we would have done it.

QUESTIONS FOR REFLECTION

1. How can I contribute to the upbuilding of the church?
2. Why must consideration be given to outsiders in determining our church practices?

3. What must be the overriding goal of worship, regardless of styles and forms?

4. How can we account for the fact that some gifted people are very difficult to live with, work for, or work with?

1 Corinthians 15:1–58

The Resurrection

CORINTH WAS A GREEK city, and due to the prevalent philosophy of that day, many of its inhabitants did not believe in the bodily resurrection of the dead. The human body was considered to be a prison and, as such, death was actually welcomed as deliverance from bondage. When Paul preached at Athens and declared the fact of Christ's resurrection, some of his listeners actually laughed at him (Acts 17:32). It appeared that the skepticism which was in the Corinthian society has spilled over to the believing community, some of whom were now denying the resurrection (v. 12), apparently due to their inability to conceive of the way in which any kind of bodily existence could be possible after death (v. 35). Hence, in this chapter, Paul presents a detailed explanation and a spirited defense of the teaching on the resurrection of Christ and the future bodily resurrection of believers. For Paul, the resurrection had important doctrinal and ethical implications for life that were too important to ignore. As such, he affirmed both the essential corporeal nature of the resurrection and its futurity. Paul dealt with the subject by answering four basic questions: are the dead raised, when are they raised, why are they raised, and how are they raised? Paul answers these questions by moving through basic steps: a recall of the basic proclamation about Jesus' resurrection (vv. 1–11), an affirmation of the logical inconsistencies involved in a denial of the resurrection (vv. 12–34), and an attempt to perceive theologically what the nature of the resurrected body must be (vv. 35–58). Paul shows that a denial of the resurrection is not only a contradiction to their own profession, but also destroys the very foundations of their faith.

THE RESURRECTION

THE RESURRECTION OF CHRIST (15:1-11)

> 1 Now I make known to you, brethren, the gospel which I preached to you, which also you received, in which also you stand,
>
> 2 by which also you are saved, if you hold fast the word which I preached to you, unless you believed in vain.
>
> 3 For I delivered to you as of first importance what I also received, that Christ died for our sins according to the Scriptures,
>
> 4 and that He was buried, and that He was raised on the third day according to the Scriptures,
>
> 5 and that He appeared to Cephas, then to the twelve.
>
> 6 After that He appeared to more than five hundred brethren at one time, most of whom remain until now, but some have fallen asleep;
>
> 7 then He appeared to James, then to all the apostles;
>
> 8 and last of all, as to one untimely born, He appeared to me also.
>
> 9 For I am the least of the apostles, and not fit to be called an apostle, because I persecuted the church of God.
>
> 10 But by the grace of God I am what I am, and His grace toward me did not prove vain; but I labored even more than all of them, yet not I, but the grace of God with me.
>
> 11 Whether then *it was* I or they, so we preach and so you believed.

Paul starts by reminding the Corinthians of the basic truth of the gospel, which was the very foundation on which the faith of the Corinthians was built. They responded to the gospel and were standing in it.

Paul's comment was extremely crucial. In recent years, scholars have argued that the resurrection of Jesus cannot be regarded as a historical event. Nothing can be farther from the truth. The fact is, that there would be no Easter faith without the historical fact of the resurrection. Without the resurrection as a fact of history, the Christian faith is empty and worthless, no matter what personal value it might hold.

THE RESURRECTION OF CHRIST (15:12-20)

> 12 Now if Christ is preached, that He has been raised from the dead, how do some among you say that there is no resurrection of the dead?
>
> 13 But if there is no resurrection of the dead, not even Christ has been raised;

1 CORINTHIANS

> 14 and if Christ has not been raised, then our preaching is vain, your faith also is vain.
>
> 15 Moreover we are even found *to be* false witnesses of God, because we testified against God that He raised Christ, whom He did not raise, if in fact the dead are not raised.
>
> 16 For if the dead are not raised, not even Christ has been raised;
>
> 17 and if Christ has not been raised, your faith is worthless; you are still in your sins.
>
> 18 Then those also who have fallen asleep in Christ have perished.
>
> 19 If we have hoped in Christ in this life only, we are of all men most to be pitied.
>
> 20 But now Christ has been raised from the dead, the first fruits of those who are asleep.

Paul begins with the question of resurrection in general—"some of you say that there is no resurrection of the dead" (v. 12b). But, he reasons, if there is no resurrection of the dead, Christ has not been raised; and, if Christ has not been raised, three conclusions of devastating consequence for the Christian life must follow. First, there is no gospel. He says, "if Christ has not been raised, our preaching is useless and so is your faith. More than that, we are then found to be false witnesses about God, for we have testified about God that he raised Christ from the dead. But he did not raise him if in fact the dead are not raised" (vv. 14–15). It stands to reason that if Christ has not been raised, every preacher, teacher, missionary in the world is—willfully or ignorantly—perpetrating a hoax, perpetuating an error and misleading people to trust in a delusion, not simply with respect to the resurrection as a fact of history, but with regard to the gospel that depends on it.

Therefore, without the resurrection of Christ as a historical fact, the Christian gospel is merely "the opiate of the people," a sort of "pie in the sky when you die" that provides smug satisfaction but has no substance. Second, there is no salvation. Paul goes on, "if Christ has not been raised, your faith is futile; you are still in your sins" (v. 17). If Christ has not been raised, then every person who has trusted in Christ for the forgiveness of sins and, on the basis of faith in Christ, has been assured that his or her sins are forgiven is in fact miserably deluded—"you are still in your sins." You have not received forgiveness. Your guilt remains. You thought you had found the way of peace and reconciliation—how wrong you were! Third, if there is no resurrection, there is no hope. Paul continues, "Then those also who have fallen asleep in Christ are lost. If only for this life we have hope in Christ, we are to be pitied more than all men" (vv. 18–19).

If Christ has not been raised, there is nothing beyond the grave. The rigors and denials of this life have been for nothing. The greatest hopes and aspirations of this life have been for nothing. If we have had hope for this life only, with no reason to expect anything after this life (as would be the case if Christ has not risen from the dead), what a pitiable state we are in! "But Christ has indeed been raised from the dead, the firstfruits of those who have fallen asleep" (v. 20). What a tremendous significance the resurrection has for the Christian! We have good news—for ourselves, for our fellows, for the whole world! All who believe in Christ can be certain of forgiveness of sins! The hope of an even fuller life beyond the grave is strong and solid! The firstfruits were an offering, not only as representative of the entire harvest that was to come, but it was also a testimony that there would be a harvest. In other words, there was more to come. It is in this sense that Jesus is declaring by his resurrection that we will also be raised, those of us who have fallen asleep (or died) in the Lord.

ASSURANCE OF BELIEVERS' RESURRECTION (15:21–22)

> 21 For since by a man *came* death, by a man also *came* the resurrection of the dead.
>
> 22 For as in Adam all die, so also in Christ all will be made alive.

Death came upon all humanity as a result of the fall of Adam. It is because all die in Adam that we need both a spiritual and bodily rebirth, and it is in Christ that all will be made alive. All who have received the gift of salvation from the Redeemer will be given this glorified resurrection body designed to never die again. It is a new kind of body, as we will see later in this chapter. It is designed to contain the new life of the one who has been born again. Remember, there were resurrections before Jesus. We read about them in the Old Testament, as well as in the New. Jesus himself raised people—the son of the widow of Nain, Jairus's daughter, and Lazarus. He raised them from the dead in the sense that he brought their old bodies back to life. But all of them eventually died again. Jesus was raised never to die. And we shall likewise be raised never to die again.

THE ORDER AND IMPORTANCE OF RESURRECTION (15:23–34)

> 23 But each in his own order: Christ the first fruits, after that those who are Christ's at His coming,
>
> 24 then *comes* the end, when He hands over the kingdom to the God and Father, when He has abolished all rule and all authority and power.
>
> 25 For He must reign until He has put all His enemies under His feet.
>
> 26 The last enemy that will be abolished is death.
>
> 27 For He has put all things in subjection under His feet. But when He says, "All things are put in subjection," it is evident that He is excepted who put all things in subjection to Him.
>
> 28 When all things are subjected to Him, then the Son Himself also will be subjected to the One who subjected all things to Him, so that God may be all in all.
>
> 29 Otherwise, what will those do who are baptized for the dead? If the dead are not raised at all, why then are they baptized for them?
>
> 30 Why are we also in danger every hour?
>
> 31 I affirm, brethren, by the boasting in you which I have in Christ Jesus our Lord, I die daily.
>
> 32 If from human motives I fought with wild beasts at Ephesus, what does it profit me? If the dead are not raised, let us eat and drink, for tomorrow we die
>
> 33 Do not be deceived: "Bad company corrupts good morals."
>
> 34 Become sober-minded as you ought, and stop sinning; for some have no knowledge of God. I speak *this* to your shame.

Not only did Jesus rise from the dead in order to redeem us from sin, but he rose to deliver us from death. There will come a time when death itself will be defeated. We are between the first Easter of Christ's resurrection and the second Easter of our resurrection. But that second Easter will come. Christ has guaranteed it by being the firstfruits. It will be when he comes that those who belong to him will receive their resurrection. He is referring here to the resurrection of the righteous, or those who believe in Jesus Christ and have given their lives to him. Those who belong to Christ could rejoice in anticipation of the resurrection. The first time he came, he came as a lamb to be sacrificed. When he comes again, he will come as a lion to conquer. He will take back what is his—namely everything. He will come again to reign until he has put all his enemies under his feet. Paul goes on to use his own lifestyle as an illustration, as well as to make a forceful statement of his conviction about the certainty of the resurrection. Many times his life was imperiled. The resurrection served as an anchor to him in the midst of the dangers that he encountered. Paul concludes with a piece of advice with reference to those who continued to deny the resurrection. The Corinthians were to dissociate from them. False teachers should be avoided because, although they claimed great knowledge, they were in fact ignorant of God.

THE RESURRECTION BODY (15:35–58)

> 35 But someone will say, "How are the dead raised? And with what kind of body do they come?"
>
> 36 You fool! That which you sow does not come to life unless it dies;
>
> 37 and that which you sow, you do not sow the body which is to be, but a bare grain, perhaps of wheat or of something else.
>
> 38 But God gives it a body just as He wished, and to each of the seeds a body of its own.
>
> 39 All flesh is not the same flesh, but there is one *flesh* of men, and another flesh of beasts, and another flesh of birds, and another of fish.
>
> 40 There are also heavenly bodies and earthly bodies, but the glory of the heavenly is one, and the *glory* of the earthly is another.
>
> 41 There is one glory of the sun, and another glory of the moon, and another glory of the stars; for star differs from star in glory.
>
> 42 So also is the resurrection of the dead. It is sown a perishable *body*, it is raised an imperishable *body*;
>
> 43 it is sown in dishonor, it is raised in glory; it is sown in weakness, it is raised in power;
>
> 44 it is sown a natural body, it is raised a spiritual body. If there is a natural body, there is also a spiritual *body*.
>
> 45 So also it is written, "The first man, Adam, became a living soul." The last Adam *became* a life-giving spirit.
>
> 46 However, the spiritual is not first, but the natural; then the spiritual.
>
> 47 The first man is from the earth, earthy; the second man is from heaven.
>
> 48 As is the earthy, so also are those who are earthy; and as is the heavenly, so also are those who are heavenly.

1 CORINTHIANS

49 Just as we have borne the image of the earthy, we will also bear the image of the heavenly.

50 Now I say this, brethren, that flesh and blood cannot inherit the kingdom of God; nor does the perishable inherit the imperishable.

51 Behold, I tell you a mystery; we will not all sleep, but we will all be changed,

52 in a moment, in the twinkling of an eye, at the last trumpet; for the trumpet will sound, and the dead will be raised imperishable, and we will be changed.

53 For this perishable must put on the imperishable, and this mortal must put on immortality.

54 But when this perishable will have put on the imperishable, and this mortal will have put on immortality, then will come about the saying that is written, "Death is swallowed up in victory.

55 O death, where is your victory? O death, where is your sting?"

56 The sting of death is sin, and the power of sin is the law;

57 but thanks be to God, who gives us the victory through our Lord Jesus Christ.

58 Therefore, my beloved brethren, be steadfast, immovable, always abounding in the work of the Lord, knowing that your toil is not *in* vain in the Lord.

One objection to belief in bodily resurrection might be its incomprehensibility. Obviously, they were referring to whether God was going to just pull back together our old bodies. This was the point of their questions. Paul, however, thinks it is foolish. All around them was evidence to the contrary, even in nature. Our old bodies must die. His contempt for their thinking is shown in his response: "How foolish!" He then proceeds to make an illustration from nature to show that belief in the resurrection was like belief in seedtime and harvest. Neither could be completely understood, but both were real. As a plant which sprouted from a seed was directly linked to it but remarkably different from it; so too was the relationship of a natural and a resurrected body. Even a seed planted in the ground must degenerate, or die, in order for the new and better life to come forth. It retains the same nature. A seed of corn does not become an oak tree, but it does not become simply a bigger seed either. Believers will have a new body (vv. 35–38). Furthermore, believers will be fitted for eternity. Not only will we have a new body, but also the new body will be fitted for eternity. Unlike the body we currently have, which is made for this world, our new resurrection bodies are going to be made for the new dimension of eternity. This is the point of the illustration that Paul is giving us in verses 30–42. He says that all flesh is not the same. And then he lists different kinds of living creatures: men, animals, birds, and fish. He mentions heavenly bodies and earthly bodies, the sun, moon, and stars. He says that each star differs from star in splendor, going on to say that the resurrection will be like that. What does he mean? God created everything uniquely designed for its purpose. Fish swim in water, while birds fly in the air. A fish would have a hard time flying, and likewise would birds find swimming underwater difficult. God created some things to live on earth, and other things to exist in the vacuum of space, and everything is unique and different. Everything is perfectly suited for what it was created for. We will be fitted for eternity in our new bodies.

One of the glorious realities of our resurrection bodies is that we will be new and better. Believers will rise again with a new body that will be improved and better in many ways. We see in our text several important contrasts that bear this out. Using the analogy of the seed sown into the ground, Paul points out the differences between our old bodies and our new and better ones. The body that is sown is perishable, and it is raised imperishable. Our human body is not made to last forever. After Adam, the head of the human race, chose to rebel against God and eat of the fruit of the tree of the knowledge of good and evil, Adam and Eve were no longer permitted to eat of the tree of life. One of the consequences of this rebellion was death. Death entered into the world and everyone is subject to it. As we saw in our last study, the last enemy to be destroyed is death. So our human body is slowly running down and will eventually die, no matter how much we exercise and eat right and take care of ourselves. Unless Jesus returns, every one of us will die. It is just a question of when. The new resurrection body, on the other hand, will never die. It is imperishable. It is made to last forever. Apparently, the laws of physics have been suspended in this new realm. Paul also states that our bodies are sown in dishonor but raised in glory.

The final reality about the resurrection that we need to understand is that we will be like Christ. Adam became a living being, and, as the first man, became the head and representative of the human race. Unfortunately, because of their rebellion against God, we receive a fallen human nature that is tainted by sin. Jesus Christ is the last Adam. He came to do what the first Adam could not do: obey God. Of course, Jesus was from heaven, and so did not inherit the sinful human nature of the first Adam. He was God made flesh. As such, his sacrifice for sin was sufficient to satisfy the divine justice of God for the entire human race. And those of us who receive that gift of grace are destined to bear the likeness of the man from heaven, just as we have borne the likeness of the earthly man. So our resurrection bodies will be like the body Jesus had.

Paul concludes the chapter on a positive note. Believers must abound in the work of the Lord, fully assured that their labor will not be in vain, but will ultimately win the victory with Christ who overcomes all things. The tomb did not mark the end of Christ's life. Neither would it mark the end of those who belong to him. Hallelujah!

QUESTIONS FOR PERSONAL REFLECTION

1. What practical significance does a future resurrection hold for you today?
2. Reflect on your service for the Lord in the light of the resurrection. Is your service half-hearted or wholehearted?
3. Think about it. What if Christ did not really rise? What hope would you have?
4. What is the difference between reincarnation and the resurrection?

1 Corinthians 16:1–24

Finance and Farewell

SOMEONE ONCE SAID THAT "Money talks—it says bye-bye." There is probably some truth to that statement. Everyone, rich or poor, has to deal with money, and how we deal with it speaks volumes about us. Money does talk. It speaks about us, our relationship with God, and what we value. What does money say about you? For Paul, this was not an option. The Corinthian Christians were responsible for taking an offering among themselves for the needs of the poor Christians of Jerusalem. They could not say that "Money is unspiritual. We will just pray for them." Paul is responding to a question that had been raised in the letter that the Corinthians had sent to him about the collection that had been organized as a special offering for the poor among God's people, especially the saints in Jerusalem. There was a great need there, and Paul was pulling together money from various churches to help them.

THE COLLECTION (16:1–4)

> 1 Now concerning the collection for the saints, as I directed the churches of Galatia, so do you also.
> 2 On the first day of every week each one of you is to put aside and save, as he may prosper, so that no collections be made when I come.
> 3 When I arrive, whomever you may approve, I will send them with letters to carry your gift to Jerusalem;
> 4 and if it is fitting for me to go also, they will go with me.

Believers must recognize that giving is as much an act of worship as singing, praying, serving, or receiving God's word through teaching. And no one is excluded. It is for everyone. In fact, he says that each one of you is to be involved in setting aside a sum of money. Of course, he is speaking directly about the contribution being collected for the poor saints in Jerusalem, but he is asking them to do that as a part of their regular giving on the Lord's Day. In other words, he was asking them to bring these special offerings to be set aside at church rather than at home.

How much should we give? Well, it depends on what we are talking about. Here Paul was talking about a special collection that was being set aside for the poor saints in Jerusalem. I am sure that he expected each person to pray about how much they were to give considering the blessing of God in their life. When he encourages them to give in keeping with his income, he is asking them to consider just how much God has blessed them. The idea here is of proportionate giving.

The purpose of giving is that God's work can be accomplished. While the streets of heaven may be paved with gold, down here on earth it takes some of that gold to pay the bills that are produced in advancing the kingdom of God, preaching the gospel to the world, and ministering to the people of God. In other words, there is always a great need. The purpose of giving is to meet that need to accomplish God's work. And to do that great work, it takes money. A very important principle of giving can be inferred from verses 3–4. It is the principle of being accountable to use God's money in a responsible way. Paul talks about giving letters of introduction to the men the Corinthians approve, who will personally take the gift and present it to the church in Jerusalem. In other words, as we give through the local church, there is a measure of accountability for how the money is used. As Christians, we should take greater precautions against being accused of mismanaging God's money.

God's plan for giving is that it should be church-centered, regular, for everyone, purposeful, proportionate, and carefully handled. That does not happen by accident. We're not to give because we have been manipulated emotionally, or pressured personally. Our giving must be loving, premeditated obedience to God's word and will, giving liberally and even sacrificially at times, to see needs met and the kingdom work of the church, the only institution Jesus established, extended and expanded. Money talks. Your giving talks. What does it say about you?

Finance and Farewell

PAUL'S TRAVEL PLANS (16:5–12)

> 5 But I will come to you after I go through Macedonia, for I am going through Macedonia;
>
> 6 and perhaps I will stay with you, or even spend the winter, so that you may send me on my way wherever I may go.
>
> 7 For I do not wish to see you now *just* in passing; for I hope to remain with you for some time, if the Lord permits.
>
> 8 But I will remain in Ephesus until Pentecost;
>
> 9 for a wide door for effective *service* has opened to me, and there are many adversaries.
>
> 10 Now if Timothy comes, see that he is with you without cause to be afraid, for he is doing the Lord's work, as I also am.
>
> 11 So let no one despise him. But send him on his way in peace, so that he may come to me; for I expect him with the brethren.
>
> 12 But concerning Apollos our brother, I encouraged him greatly to come to you with the brethren; and it was not at all *his* desire to come now, but he will come when he has opportunity.

"If the Lord permits:"; Paul leaves all his plans up to the will of the Lord. He planned to go through the region of Macedonia, visiting Corinth. But things happened differently than he had planned. Instead of what he had planned, Paul made a painful visit to Corinth to personally confront them in some areas. Although believers must plan and do things in orderly fashion, they must leave room for God's interference. Paul knew that his schedule was not his alone to make. He knew he could only follow his plan if the Lord permitted. He was a man who knew that he was serving God's purposes, not his own, and so he needed to remain flexible to the leading of the Spirit as to the timing of what he was called to do. We need both vision and flexibility. Paul wisely relied not only on his own desires, but also on God's open doors. Paul knew the secret of directed service. He says that a great door for effective work has opened to him, and so he had decided to stay at Ephesus in order to take advantage of that opportunity. But Paul also knew that opposition often accompanies opportunities. What a great lesson for all believers, especially Christian ministers.

Paul mentions the impending visits of two of his trusted fellow workers, Timothy and Apollos. Timothy, Paul's mentee, was the one carrying on the work of the Lord together with Paul, and Paul vouches for Timothy's integrity, instructing the Corinthians to receive him well and then send him on his way in peace. Paul is expecting him to return along with the brothers, obviously other coworkers. Then he turns his attention to Apollos, who they knew as one who had ministered among them. Even though Paul had strongly urged him to go to see them, apparently Apollos was quite unwilling to drop everything and go and that time. In other words, he said no. Apparently, we do not have to say yes to everything people want us to do. Again, we see their flexibility.

PARTING EXHORTATIONS (16:13–14)

> 13 Be on the alert, stand firm in the faith, act like men, be strong.
> 14 Let all that you do be done in love.

In verses 13 and 14, Paul exhorts believers to be on their guard. They must never forget that there is a spiritual enemy, Satan, who is relentless, prowling about like a lion seeking whom he may devour. Paul says, Do not forget. Be vigilant. Stay awake. Additionally, we are to stand firm in the faith. Dig in, and do not let anything move you away from what you know to be true. Knowing that we are in a battle, we must be men and women of courage. It will take courage. Remember, courage does not mean the absence of fear. Courage is doing what you know you need to do in spite of fear. That is why we are told to be strong. As Adam Clarke notes, the terms in this verse are all military:

> Watch ye, watch, and be continually on your guard, lest you be surprised by your enemies . . . Stand fast in the faith—Keep in your ranks; do not be disorderly; be determined to keep your ranks unbroken; keep close together . . . Quit yourselves like men—When you are attacked, do not flinch; maintain your ground; resist; press forward; strike home; keep compact; conquer . . . Be strong—If one company or division be opposed by too great a force of the enemy, strengthen that division, and maintain your position . . . summon up all your courage, sustain each other; fear not, for fear will enervate you.[1]

We cannot afford to forget that we are in a war. But we must also remember that it is a spiritual battle.

---

1. Clarke, *Romans–Revelation*, 93.

Finance and Farewell

CONCLUDING GREETINGS (16:15–24)

> 15 Now I urge you, brethren (you know the household of Stephanas, that they were the first fruits of Achaia, and that they have devoted themselves for ministry to the saints),
>
> 16 that you also be in subjection to such men and to everyone who helps in the work and labors.
>
> 17 I rejoice over the coming of Stephanas and Fortunatus and Achaicus, because they have supplied what was lacking on your part.
>
> 18 For they have refreshed my spirit and yours. Therefore acknowledge such men.
>
> 19 The churches of Asia greet you. Aquila and Prisca greet you heartily in the Lord, with the church that is in their house.
>
> 20 All the brethren greet you. Greet one another with a holy kiss.
>
> 21 The greeting is in my own hand—Paul.
>
> 22 If anyone does not love the Lord, he is to be accursed. Maranatha.
>
> 23 The grace of the Lord Jesus be with you.
>
> 24 My love be with you all in Christ Jesus. Amen.

As Paul ends this letter to the church in Corinth, he mentions a number of individuals who were his coworkers and to whom he wanted to give recognition. This, of course, was his common practice in ending all of his letters. Often, however, we are tempted to skip over this list of individuals as if it were just a routine practice, and has no practical teaching value for us. But this is not true. One of the most profound statements it makes to us as individuals is that we do not live the Christian life individualistically. While each individual must make his or her own individual commitment to Christ, we are then called to live out that commitment in the context of Christian community. Our lives were never meant to be lived in isolation.

Paul makes it clear that as believers we are interdependent. As Christians, we are called to work together in the common cause of sharing the message of Christ with the whole world. It takes more than a few talented individuals to get the job done. It is so easy for us to focus on the "superstars" of Christianity. In fact, this was one of the very problems they were experiencing in Corinth. People were taking sides, following their favorite "star" preacher. Some were "of Paul," while others were "of Apollos," and still others were "of Cephas" (Peter). If we are to see what God can really do, there must be a recognition of our interdependence in the body of Christ.

1 CORINTHIANS

Notice the people he mentions in the remainder of this chapter. He is not merely mentioning people at random. He is pointing out those who have been part of the team that made the work possible.

Paul ends the letter with some wishes. For Paul, love for the Lord is a mark of a true Christian. Such was his deep conviction that he pronounces a curse on whoever does not love the Lord. So, first, he says, "let anyone be accursed who has no love for the Lord." Second, he expresses a sentiment that was common to the early church: "Come Lord Jesus." Paul's third wish is that the grace of our Lord Jesus be with the Corinthians, as he concludes the letter with the expression of his love for the Corinthians.

QUESTIONS FOR PERSONAL REFLECTION

1. Why is it important for the church to be involved in meeting the need of others? How often should it be done? How much should Christians give for the need of others?

2. Should Christians be involved in relief work? Why or why not? Does your church have regular programs or funds to care and provide for the needy?

3. What is my Christian responsibility to believers and churches in other places where the members are suffering or facing persecution?

4. What do we learn about accountability from the way Paul managed the collection for the Jerusalem saints?

Further Reading

Adewuya, J. Ayodeji. *A Commentary on 1 & 2 Corinthians*. SPCK International Study Guide 42. London: SPCK, 2009.
Barnett, Paul. *1 Corinthians: Holiness and Hope of a Rescued People*. Focus on the Bible. Ross-shire: Christian Focus, 2000.
Barrett, C. K. *A Commentary on the First Epistle to the Corinthians*. Harper's New Testament Commentaries. Peabody: Hendrickson, 1968.
———. *The First Epistle to the Corinthians*. Black's New Testament Commentaries. London: Black, 1971.
Barth, Karl. *The Resurrection of the Dead*. Translated by H. J. Stenning. London: Hodder & Stoughton, 1933.
Beet, Joseph Agar. *A Commentary on St. Paul's Epistles to the Corinthians: Volume 1, First Corinthians*. Salem: Schmul, 1988.
Belleville, Linda L. *2 Corinthians*. The InterVarsity Press New Testament Commentary Series 8. Downers Grove: InterVarsity, 1996.
Bruce, F. F. *I and II Corinthians*. The New Century Bible Commentary. Grand Rapids: Eerdmans, 1971.
Clarke, Adam. *Clarke's Commentary, Vol. 6: Romans–Revelation*. Clarke's Commentary. Nashville: Abingdon, nd.
Crocker, Cornelia Cyss. *Reading 1 Corinthians in the Twenty-First Century*. New York: T. & T. Clark International, 2004.
Ellingworth, Paul, and Howard A. Hatton. *A Handbook on Paul's First Letter to the Corinthians*. United Bible Society Handbook Series. New York: United Bible Society, 1995.
Fee, Gordon D. *The First Epistle to the Corinthians*. The New International Commentary on the New Testament. Grand Rapids: Eerdmans, 1987.
Garland, David E. *1 Corinthians*. Baker Exegetical Commentary on the New Testament. Grand Rapids: Baker Academic, 2003.
Hargreaves, John. *A Guide to 1 Corinthians*. TEF Study Guide 17. London: SPCK, 1978.
Harris, Murray J. *The Second Epistle to the Corinthians: A Commentary on the Greek Text*. New International Greek Testament Commentary. Grand Rapids: Eerdmans, 2005.
Hays, Richard B. *First Corinthians*. Interpretation: A Bible Commentary for Teaching and Preaching. Louisville: John Knox, 1997.
Hughes, Robert B. *First Corinthians*. Everyman's Bible Commentary. Chicago: Moody Press, 1985.

Further Reading

Johnson, Alan F. *1 Corinthians*. The InterVarsity Press New Testament Commentary Series. Downers Grove: InterVarsity, 2004.
Keener, Craig S. *1-2 Corinthians*. New Cambridge Bible Commentory. Cambridge: Cambridge University Press, 2005.
Lull, David J. *1 Corinthians*. Chalice Commentaries for Today. St. Louis: Chalice Press, 2007.
Martin, Ralph P. *1-2 Corinthians*. Word Biblical Themes. Dallas: Word, 1988.
———. *II Corinthians*. Word Biblical Commentary 40. Waco: Word, 1986.
Morgan, G. Campbell. *The Corinthian Letters of Paul: An Exposition of I and II Corinthians*. Westwood: Revell, 1946.
Morris, Leon. *1 Corinthians*. Tyndale New Testeament Commentaries 7. Grand Rapids: InterVarsity, 1985.
Murphy-O'Connor, Jerome. *1 Corinthians*. The People's Bible Commentary. Rev. ed. Oxford: Bible Reading Fellowship, 1997.
Orr, William F., and James Arthur Walther. *I Corinthians*. Anchor Bible 32. New York: Doubleday, 1976.
Pascuzzi, Maria A. *First and Second Corinthians*. New Collegeville Bible Commentary: New Testament 7. Collegeville: Liturgical, 2005.
Plummer, Alfred. *A Critical and Exegetical Commentary on the Second Epistle of St. Paul to the Corinthians*. The International Critical Commentary on the Holy Scriptures of the Old and New Testaments 34. Edinburgh: T. & T. Clark, 1985.
Robertson, Archibald, and Alfred Plummer. *A Critical and Exegetical Commentary on the First Epistle of St. Paul to the Corinthians*. The International Critical Commentary on the Holy Scriptures of the Old and New Testaments 33. Edinburgh: T. & T. Clark, 1986.
Schenck, Kenneth. *1 and 2 Corinthians: A Commentary for Bible Students*. Wesleyan Bible Commentary Series. Indianapolis: Wesleyan, 2006.
Scott, James M. *2 Corinthians*. New International Biblical Commentary: New Testament Series 6. Peabody: Paternoster, 1998.
Talbert, Charles H. *Reading Corinthians: A Literary and Theological Commentary on 1 and 2 Corinthians*. Reading the New Testament Series. London: SPCK, 1987.
Thiselton, Anthony C. *1 Corinthians: A Shorter Exegetical & Pastoral Commentary*. Grand Rapids: Eerdmans, 2006.
Watson, Nigel. *The First Epistle to the Corinthians*. Epworth Commentaries. London: Epworth, 1992.
Welch, W. Wilbert. *Conduct Becoming Saints: The Book of 1 Corinthians: Part 1, Chapters 1-8*. Edited by Merle R. Hull. Schaumburg: Regular Baptist, 1978.
Willoughby, W. Robert. *First Corinthians: Fostering Spirituality*. The Deeper Life Pulpit Commentary. Camp Hill: Christian Publications, 1984.
Wilson, Geoffrey B. *2 Corinthians: A Digest of Reformed Comment*. Edinburgh: Banner of Truth Trust, 1979.
Witherington, Ben, III. *Conflict & Community in Corinth: A Social-Rhetorical Commentary on 1 and 2 Corinthians*. Grand Rapids: Eerdmans, 1995.

www.ingramcontent.com/pod-product-compliance
Lightning Source LLC
Chambersburg PA
CBHW072148160426
43197CB00012B/2288